Contents

Preface

The first edition of this book was called simply *Equity and efficiency*. Now the title of this second edition has been lengthened to fit the new syllabuses. There are two completely new chapters, both of which are central to equity, efficiency and market failure – namely, supply side reforms and the welfare state.

Simply peruse the Introduction of this short book and you will realize that the author covers all these topics in a very convincing and interesting way.

This volume now contains both the theory and applied microeconomics of the new SCAA 'core' for A and AS levels.

Bryan Hurl
Series Editor

Introduction

There are two principal criteria by which economic outcomes are judged: equity and efficiency. Efficiency is achieved if the output from an economy's resources is at a maximum *and* if this output is that which yields the greatest satisfaction, or utility, to consumers. In *Chapter 1* there is a precise definition of efficiency which includes a discussion of the concept of Pareto efficiency. Chapter 1 also discusses equity, which is more difficult to define. It requires that there should be a fair distribution of welfare – that is, a fair distribution of the economy's goods and services. But there is no objective measure of fairness. For one person it is fair that those who put in the effort get the rewards, with only subsistence incomes for the rest. Another person would judge this to be most unfair.

Chapters 2 to 8 apply the ideas of equity and efficiency to a variety of economic issues. We find that frequently there is conflict between the two principles. For example, taxing workers' incomes to pay unemployment benefits may reduce the incentive to work. However, such conflict is not always the case: regulating monopoly or taxing polluters can be both efficient and fair.

Chapter 2 is about economic systems. The market system is efficient but inequitable; planning is inefficient but has the potential to be fair. However, the inefficiencies of the command economy appear to overwhelm any equity advantages and recently many planned economies have been rejected by their citizens, and an urgent task is to help them to develop efficient market systems.

Chapters 3 and 4 compare competition and monopoly. Chapter 3 focuses on theory and Chapter 4 on policy. In Chapter 3 we discover that competition is efficient, and that monopoly is both inefficient (there is under-production) and unfair (consumers are exploited). However, the inefficiency argument is based on fairly restrictive assumptions, whereas in the real world monopoly may lead to lower costs, to innovation and to economic growth. If this happens, consumers benefit.

Chapter 4 shows that British competition policy starts from the premise that the issue of monopoly is not clear-cut and that each case must be judged on its merits. The costs of monopoly are balanced against its potential benefits in terms of economies of scale, research and development, long-run growth and strength in international markets. There is a lot of criticism of UK policy where the aim is to *regulate* monopoly. It contrasts with the US approach which starts with the assumption that monopoly power is always bad and should be broken up.

Chapter 5 is about external costs, for example pollution and the greenhouse effect. External costs are both unfair, because they are imposed on third parties, and inefficient, because they reduce total welfare. There is no policy conflict between equity and efficiency.

Chapter 6 defines and gives examples of external benefits. Goods that confer these benefits are produced in less than efficient quantities by the market, and we discover why this happens. The benefits of some goods are *all* external: these are public goods. Other goods provide both internal (private) and external benefits and so are known as mixed goods. Chapter 6 discusses both public and mixed goods, and the role the government plays in providing them.

Chapter 7 is about the supply side of the economy and about supply side policies. Here there can be conflict between efficiency and equity. Trying to boost the supply side – to raise employment and output – may mean choosing policies to raise in-work incomes and reduce out-of-work incomes (lower income taxes and lower benefits). It can lead to free market policies which abolish wages councils that protect low earners, which weaken the powers of trades unions, and which implement privatization. The consequences of these policies is to increase income differentials both before and after taxation. There *may* be higher output, but the cost is more inequality.

Chapter 8 discusses the economics of the welfare state. There is a brief account of health care, education and housing which were discussed in terms of equity and efficiency issues in Chapter 6. The main focus of this chapter is social security – cash transfer payments – and the conflicts between equity and efficiency which afflict the social security system. Efficiency requires economic incentives (to work), equity requires that those out of work receive money from the state to support themselves and their families. The unemployment and poverty traps are discussed and it becomes clear that the latter, in particular, is a fairly intractable problem. The chapter concludes with a brief outline of the debate on the future of social security.

Chapter One

Equity and efficiency

'And the moral of that is – "The more there is of mine the less there is of yours." *"Oh, I know," exclaimed Alice, who had not attended to this last remark.'* Lewis Carroll

Scarcity and choice

In all economies, people's wants for goods and services are unlimited but the resources to satisfy them are scarce. Choices must therefore be made about what goods and services to produce, how to produce them, and who should get them. Any economic system must undertake two functions, **allocation** and **distribution:**

- Resources must be allocated to the production of goods and services – to answer the *what?* and *how?* questions.
- Output must be distributed among consumers – there must be a solution to the *for whom?* question.

It is a goal of economic policy that allocation should be efficient and distribution should be equitable.

- **Efficiency** is concerned with resource allocation. It is achieved by maximizing consumers' economic welfare within a given income distribution.
- **Equity** is about how income should be distributed, and is more difficult to define as there is no consensus on what is a fair outcome – *'... equity, like beauty, is in the mind of the beholder'* (McLachan and Maynard), or ' *"Fairness", like "needs", is in the eye of the beholder'* (Friedman).

Welfare economics

The purpose of **welfare economics** is to assess how well the economy works when judged by the criteria of both efficiency and equity. It provides us with an economic theory of **social welfare**. It includes both description and prescription. It *describes* an efficient allocation of resources – the conditions necessary to achieve maximum welfare, given the distribution pattern. It also *prescribes* – it is **normative**, in particular on distribution.

Efficiency

There are different ways of defining efficiency. An engineer thinks of efficiency as maximizing output from given inputs. This amounts to the production of goods and services at minimum cost in terms of resources, which is **productive efficiency** (sometimes called technical efficiency). An economist defines efficiency to include demand, so that it becomes maximizing the output of goods and services *which consumers demand* at minimum resource cost. This wider concept is known as economic or **allocative efficiency**.

Allocative efficiency is also known as **Pareto efficiency**. Vilfredo Pareto (1848–1923) argued that the allocation of resources was at a social 'optimum' if it was not possible to improve one consumer's welfare without making another worse off. Efficient allocation was attained if consumer A could not be made better-off without reducing B's welfare. (Given that diagrams are two-dimensional, we assume two goods and two consumers, Figures 1 and 2.) The Pareto criterion assumes that the distribution of income is given and it has nothing to say about equity. B may be very rich and A may be very poor, but if A's welfare cannot be improved except by reducing B's then the outcome is Pareto-efficient. (This should make it clear why Hahn objects to the use of the expression '**Pareto optimum**' – see the box.) There are many Pareto-efficient allocations and each one of them represents a different distribution of welfare.

... there are many Pareto-efficient allocations and each one of them will have a different distribution of welfare. Mrs Thatcher's [1] choice of a Pareto-efficient allocation, for instance, seems unlikely to correspond to any acceptable notion of distributive justice. Mr Benn's [2] choice on the other hand may not even be Pareto-efficient. In any case, the sloppy habit in the literature in speaking of a Pareto-optimum has misled many people into believing that their duty of serious moral argument has been fulfilled when they can show that some policy outcome is Pareto-efficient. As a matter of fact this is just the beginning of such an argument.

[1] Conservative prime minister 1979–90; [2] Labour MP

Frank Hahn, 'Reflections on the invisible hand', *Lloyds Bank Review*, 1982

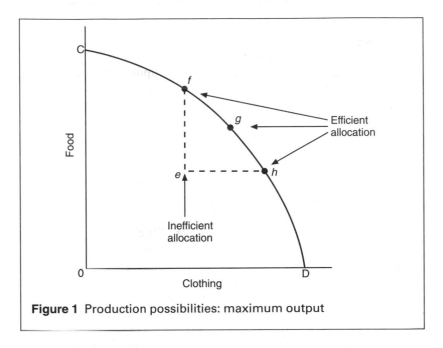

Figure 1 Production possibilities: maximum output

To attain Pareto efficiency there must be maximum output from given inputs, and maximum consumer utility from that output. Maximum output from given inputs means that productive efficiency, production of output at minimum opportunity cost, is part of allocative efficiency. Productive efficiency can be illustrated using a **production possibility curve**, as in Figure 1.

The line CD represents the maximum potential production of food and clothing. It shows that in order to have more clothing it is necessary to sacrifice some food production. It thus shows the *opportunity cost* of food in terms of clothing (and vice versa). Any point, any combination of food and clothing, on the production possibility curve CD is efficient. The quantity of each good is produced at minimum opportunity cost. Any point inside it is inefficient because production from the resources available could be increased (as far as the line CD). With given resources and technology, all points beyond CD are unattainable. Thus e is inefficient because it is possible to have more of both goods (g) or more of one good without any less of the other (f or h). At e it is possible, by increasing output, to make either or both consumers better-off without reducing the other's welfare.

Pareto efficiency also requires maximum consumer utility from the consumption of that output. This can be illustrated by a 'utility frontier', as in Figure 2. It is drawn on the assumption that production is

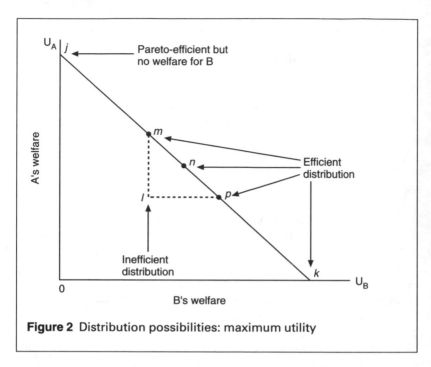

Figure 2 Distribution possibilities: maximum utility

efficient, that the economy is on the production possibility curve and that there are an infinite number of income (and hence, utility) distributions.

Every point on the frontier is Pareto-efficient (one consumer can be made better-off only if the other is made worse-off), every point inside it is inefficient. *l* is inefficient because it is possible to make A better-off without worsening B's position – a move to *m*, or to make B better-off without reducing A's welfare – a move to *p*; or, at *n*, both of them would be better-off.

The inefficient situation exists when the two consumers value the two goods differently. If A values food more highly in terms of clothing than B, and B values clothing in terms of food more highly than A, then if A gets more food (and less clothing), and B more clothing (and less food) the welfare of both is improved.

When they both put the same value on food and clothing, in terms of the alternative good forgone, distributive efficiency is achieved. Points to the left of *m* or to the right of *p* are Pareto-efficient (Pareto-'optimal') though they appear to be unfair distributions of welfare. Even *j* is Pareto-efficient, though there B's utility is zero. The distribution problem would soon be solved by B's death. There would then be a Robinson Crusoe (before Friday) economy with only the *what?* and *how?* questions to be solved, and with the only criterion for judging the outcome that of efficiency.

Equity

Equity is about **social justice** and fairness, distributional goals. In terms of Figure 2, it requires people to make judgements about what points on the welfare frontier are desirable or acceptable. It requires us to evaluate policy changes which improve some people's welfare at the cost of reducing others'. For example, how much should people be taxed in order to provide others with goods or incomes? What point on the utility frontier is fair between A and B? It comes from a set of principles about what people ought to have *as of right*. However, this does not take us very far as different people have different principles – value judgements are involved.

A person taking an individualistic libertarian approach (see the box 'Free to choose' on page 8) would argue that equity is achieved if minimum standards – for income, education, health care, and so on – are achieved. This is to regard higher standards as part of society's reward system. Those with a fraternal, collectivist philosophy are not satisfied with minimum standards. What is fair for them is income support which takes account of the average standard, and equality of access to services such as health and education, and treatment according to need. If this erodes incentives (either of taxpayers or of claimants) there will be conflicts with efficiency. We shall look at this in

"I'll be glad when we have a classless society – I never could stand the poor."

Chapter 7 on the supply side and in Chapter 8 on the welfare state.

The Friedmans' views are extreme, and their claim that 'equality of outcome' is the alternative to their ideas caricatures serious alternatives. Those who take a more fraternal view of society might argue for equality of access, and hence perhaps equality of outcome, to state-provided income in kind like health care and education. But no-one proposes equality of outcome in the provision of money incomes. There may be differences over what the level of cash support should be for those who need it, but there is no call for equal incomes for all.

Free to choose

That different concept (as compared with 'equality before God' and equality of opportunity), equality of outcome, has been gaining ground in this century. In some intellectual circles the desirability of equality of outcome has become an article of religious faith: everyone should finish the race at the same time. As the Dodo said in *Alice in Wonderland*: '*Everybody* has won, and *all* must have prizes.'

For this concept, as for the other two, 'equal' is not to be interpreted literally as 'identical'. No one really maintains that everyone, regardless of age or sex or other physical qualities, should have identical rations of each separate item of food, clothing, and so on. The goal is rather 'fairness', a much vaguer notion – indeed, one that is difficult, if not impossible, to define precisely. 'Fair shares for all' is the modern slogan that has replaced Karl Marx's 'To each according to his needs, from each according to his ability'.

This concept of equality differs radically from the other two. Government measures that promote personal equality or equality of opportunity enhance liberty; government measures to achieve 'fair shares for all' reduce liberty. If what people get is to be determined by 'fairness', who is to decide what is 'fair'? As a chorus of voices asked the Dodo, 'But who is to give the prizes?'. 'Fairness' is not an objectively determined concept once it departs from identity. 'Fairness', like 'needs', is in the eye of the beholder. If all are to have 'fair shares', someone or some group of people must decide what shares are fair – and they must be able to impose their decisions on others, taking from those who have more than their 'fair' share and giving to those who have less. Are those who make and impose such decisions equal to those for whom they decided? Are we not in George Orwell's *Animal Farm*, where 'all animals are equal, but some animals are more equal than others'?

In addition, if what people get is determined by 'fairness' and not by what they produce, where are the 'prizes' to come from? What incentive is there to work and produce? How is it to be decided who is to be the doctor, who the lawyer, who the garbage collector, who the street sweeper? What assures that people will accept the roles assigned to them and perform those roles in accordance with their abilities? Clearly, only force or the threat of force will do.

Source: *Free to Choose* by Milton and Rose Friedman, Penguin Books, 1980

Efficiency and equity are the criteria by which economic outcomes may be judged. In theory there is no problem over the definition of efficiency, though in practice there may be. Both in theory and in practice there are problems and disagreements over equity. This is because, as Lewis Carroll pointed out, 'the more there is of mine the less there is of yours'. Nevertheless the idea is used, along with efficiency, to judge how well real economies perform. This is the task we turn to in Chapter 3, after first having described alternative economic systems.

KEY WORDS

Allocation (what? how?)	Productive efficiency
Distribution (for whom?)	Allocative efficiency
Efficiency	Pareto efficiency
Equity	'Pareto optimum'
Welfare economics	Production possibility curve
Social welfare	Utility frontier
Normative	Social justice

Reading list

Anderton, A., Units 34 and 43 in *Economics*, 2nd edn, Causeway Press, 1995.

Friedman, M., and Friedman, R., Chapters 1 and 5 in *Free to Choose*, Penguin Books, 1980.

Wales, J., Chapter 10 in *Investigating Social Issues,* Macmillan, 1990.

Essay topics

1. What is meant by the term 'economic efficiency'? To what extent does the price mechanism ensure that resources are allocated efficiently?
   [University of London Examinations and Assessment Council 1990]
2. Explain what is meant by equity and efficiency and why they are important in evaluating economic systems. Is it possible for an economic system to be both equitable and efficient or must the increase in one automatically decrease the other? Illustrate your answer from recent experience. [25 marks]
   [Northern Examinations and Assessment Board 1993]
3. How can economic analysis be used to help attain an efficient allocation of resources in an economy? [25 marks]
   [University of Cambridge Local Examinations Syndicate 1996]

Chapter Two
Economic systems

' *"Would you tell me, please, which way I ought to go from here?"*
"That depends a good deal on where you want to get to," said the
Cheshire Cat.' Lewis Carroll

Markets and planning

The mechanism by which resources are allocated to the production of
output and by which output is distributed to final buyers is known as
the **economic system**. The system comprises an organization or set of
institutions: free markets constitute one such system, planning offices
operating with a central planning bureau constitute another. Thus,
economic systems can vary from, at one extreme, an unplanned free
market system to, at the other extreme, a centrally planned **command
economy**.

Neither of these extremes is to be found in the real world because
both systems have their drawbacks and weaknesses. *No economy
relies entirely on the market, and no economy has central planners to
take every single decision on what, how and for whom to produce.* A
spectrum of systems with different degrees of planning and free market
mechanisms exists; the economic system reflects the culture and values
of the society it serves.

Ownership systems: capitalism and socialism

Capitalism refers to the private ownership of an economy's productive
resources, **socialism** to social ownership. Under socialism the means of
production are communally owned; for example, a factory may be
owned by its workers, or, more usually, there is state ownership.

It is important to distinguish between an economy's *economic system* and its *ownership system*. Careless use of terms sees 'capitalism'
and 'market system' and, similarly, 'socialism' and 'planned economy'
used as if they were synonymous. They are not. Market economies,
based on competition, tend to be capitalist; and socialism, with its
cooperative philosophy, and planning have tended to go together. But
this is not inevitable. For example, during the Second World War the
UK remained capitalist but became a command economy; the government decided what and how to produce, and a rationing system
determined who would get those goods not aimed at the war effort.

Conversely, some countries which until recently have been socialist have always used markets, to a greater or lesser degree, to allocate resources.

There is, however, an argument that for market economies to work there *must* be a capitalist ownership system; and that without the profit incentive for private owners (see on) markets will not lead to efficient, cost-minimizing outcomes. This argument has been advanced particularly in the context of prescribing how eastern European economies should be reformed. It is probably correct when applied to a wholly state-owned economy, but it is unlikely to be true of a mixed economy where public enterprise and its managers are judged by the standards of private enterprise. *It does not appear that one hundred per cent of productive resources must be privately owned for an economy to be efficient.*

Nevertheless most commentators would concede that to achieve efficiency eastern European economies require market forces and privatization, particularly of those sectors of the economy which can be competitive. However, it might also be concluded that caution and selectivity might yield better outcomes than a headlong stampede to privatize everything, including natural monopolies, immediately.

In practice, all economies are a mixture of markets and planning, and there may be a mixture of capitalism and socialism. The USA, for example, is primarily a market economy, but even there the state decides on the allocation of resources to defence, education, roads, and so on, and determines the distribution of incomes and health care to the old and the poor. Conversely, in planned economies markets were given some role in directing production.

Capitalism and socialism may also be mixed, though the ownership system may be purer than the economic system. There may be pure socialism, with no private ownership of anything apart from personal possessions (an example is Albania, at least until recently); or there may be fairly pure capitalism, with private ownership of nearly all productive resources. There may also be a mixture. In France, for example – again at least until recently – there has been fairly wide state ownership, including of manufacturing companies like Renault. Until the privatization programme of the 1980s, the UK had a similarly mixed system.

The command economy

In a hypothetical, pure command (planned) economy the government would take all decisions about consumption and production – what to produce, and how, and who gets it. Consumers would not be sovereign, planners would decide what to produce. The central planners would also attempt to answer the *how?* question – they would have to take decisions on production techniques and on the capital and labour intensity of production. For developed economies, the task would be immensely complicated, even if aided by the most advanced of computers.

Planners would also determine income distribution. In a pure command economy money would not be necessary – people would receive pieces of paper giving direct entitlement to a particular quantity of specified goods and services. However, in practice in command economies people received money incomes which they were free to spend on those goods the planners decided should be produced.

Planning failure

Planning, as compared with the invisible hand of free markets, was frequently criticized for its inefficiency – in the general and the economic sense of that word. The failure of planned economies to achieve productive efficiency and to meet consumers' wants, and the recent changes in many of those economies towards the use of markets to allocate resources, shows that such criticism was well-founded. The view that planning can work as efficiently as decentralized markets has been fundamentally undermined.

The principal criticisms of the allocation of resources by planners are that production is not guided by consumer preferences, and that resources are not used in least-cost (most efficient) combinations. First, prices do not guide supply as they do in a market economy – they merely are raised or lowered to ration out what is produced. Planners may be guided to move resources because there are gluts or shortages or long order books. But the consumer can hardly be said to be sovereign. People get used to being grateful if they can find coats to buy, though really they might prefer shoes. The inefficiency of planning in meeting consumer wants becomes a particular problem as an economy develops. In Maoist China, when everyone wore an identical blue uniform, it was not difficult to plan clothing output. But economic development brings a proliferation of products, so that there are millions of different goods and services. How would a planner know how many single-serving vegetable lasagnes or colourfast orchid lipsticks to produce? (An anti-growth person might argue that these are floss and fripperies. They appear, however, to be what people want. Fortunately discussion of economic systems and individual freedoms is beyond the scope of this book.)

Even if there were only thousands rather than millions of goods, the task of coordination of production would be complex because the output of one industry represents the inputs of many others. In a capitalist market economy, firms compete with each other to make profits, and in competitive markets the profit maximization motive leads them to use least-cost methods of satisfying consumers' wants. In a planned economy, competition and the motivation to make profits are absent, despite the use of 'notional' profits. Plant managers have to reach output targets, and receive bonuses for doing so, but there is little incentive for cost minimization. Targets depend on past production, and so for a margin of safety for the future, a plant manager will keep output below capacity potential. This is inefficient. There is further waste and expense in a planning system because there is a whole hierarchy of planners (civil servants, officials) who are unavailable for other more productive work. These are the people whose jobs depend on the existence of a planning system, the people who hindered *perestroika* (restructuring) in the former USSR.

Finally, planned economies can answer the *for whom?* question potentially satisfactorily. They can be fair, there need be no-one without an income, as there is in the market economy. However, planners do not have complete freedom to distribute goods. If people are to be motivated to do all the jobs that need doing, there have to be differentials between wage incomes. But these necessary differentials need not be as great as in a market system where some differences have non-economic causes. And the large inequalities which come from property ('unearned') income will not exist if the planned economy is also socialist. Income may be more equally distributed, but average income per head may be so much less than in more efficient market economies, that the poorest, though not so far from those with average or high incomes, may still be worse off than the poor in a market system.

Whether the poor in a socialist command economy feel worse or better off than the poor in capitalist market systems depends on whether they assess their position in absolute or relative terms. There is an apocryphal story of an East German's view on the triumph of markets and capitalism: 'We only had Trabants then, but at least we all only had Trabants.' Chapter 8 has something further to say about relative poverty.

The market economy

The decision-taking units in the market economy are households, who are resource owners and consumers, and firms, who are resource users and producers. Economic agents pursue their own interests. We assume that consumers aim at maximizing their own welfare or utility, and that firms aim at maximizing profits. The government plays no part in resource allocation and distribution in a pure market economy. Prices transmit information, are incentives to action, coordinate demand and supply, and distribute income.

Figure 3 shows a model of this system. Markets and prices allocate resources and distribute output. There is private ownership of resources, so it is also a capitalist as well as a market economy.

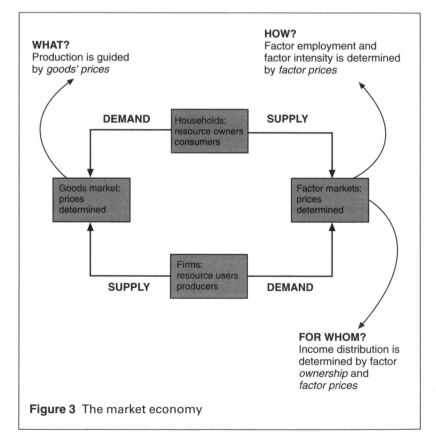

Figure 3 The market economy

Households and firms meet in the goods and factor markets. In the goods market the interaction of demand and supply determines prices, and prices inform firms what to produce. In the factor market, supply and demand determine wages, interest and rent, and these factor prices guide profit-maximizing firms to the least-cost (most efficient) combination of factors. The *how?* part of the allocation question is answered. Finally, distribution (*for whom?*): in a market economy a household's income depends on the factors it owns and the prices put on those resources in the factor market.

The price mechanism can achieve efficient – welfare-maximizing – levels of output. Figure 4 shows how this happens in the market for a single good. However, this is the result only if there is **perfect competition** and no **external effects**. For the moment we will assume that this is the situation.

Figure 4 shows market supply and demand curves obtained by summing firms' supply curves and consumers' demand curves. The supply curve of a firm in perfect competition is its marginal cost curve and the market supply curve is the sum of firms' MC curves ($S = \Sigma MC$). The

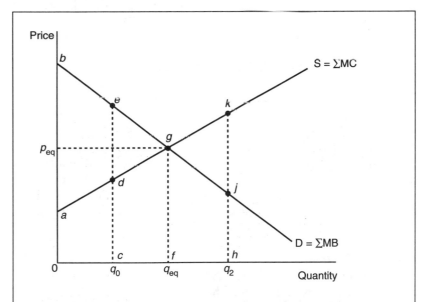

Figure 4 Welfare maximizing output achieved by the price mechanism. Each unit to the left of q_{eq} adds more to the benefits than to costs (MB > MC); each unit beyond q_{eq} adds more to costs than to benefits (MC > MB). Therefore every unit up to q_{eq} should be produced, but output should not go beyond q_{eq}

market demand curve is the sum of individual's demand curves which reflect the welfare, or benefit, obtained from consumption (D = ΣMB).

To find the optimum output for society we need to compare all the costs of production with all the benefits from consumption; that is, we need to compare **social costs** and **social benefits**. If there are no external effects (see on) then private costs and social costs are identical and the market supply curve represents social costs; similarly private and social benefits are the same, and the market demand curve represents social benefits.

Now we are in a position to see how the price mechanism achieves efficiency. For welfare to be maximized – for an efficient outcome – every unit which yields a larger benefit than it costs should be produced, and no unit which costs more than the benefits it provides should be made. This is the case at the market equilibrium, q_{eq}. Each unit between 0 and q_{eq} adds more to benefits than to costs. For example, the unit at q_0 costs cd but gives benefits of ce, so it adds de to net benefits. Every unit beyond (to the right of) q_{eq} costs more than the benefits it yields. For example, if the marginal unit at q_2 were produced it would give benefits of hj but would cost much more, hk. Production should stop at q_{eq} where marginal social cost and marginal social benefit (= fg) are exactly equal to each other. At the market equilibrium, achieved by price p_{eq}, total benefits are $0bgf$ and total costs are $0agf$; and net benefits, abg, are maximized. Hence **allocative efficiency** is achieved.

How competitive markets achieve **productive efficiency** – cost minimization – which is part of an efficient outcome, will be shown in Chapter 3 when perfect competition is compared with monopoly.

Finally, the **distributive efficiency** illustrated in Figure 2 in the previous chapter is also achieved by competitive markets. All consumers face the same set of prices. This leads each of them to get the same value (at the margin) from one good in terms of another. Within a given income distribution consumer welfare is maximized – the utility frontier is attained.

Market failure

The market achieves a welfare maximizing (efficient) outcome only when competition is perfect and when there are no external benefits or costs. Frequently this is not the case and the consequence is **market failure**.

In the real world transactors may have incomplete information and their access to markets may be limited. Where there is monopoly there is no supply curve based on costs, profit maximizing output is less than efficient output, and some units which would add more to benefits than to costs are not produced (see Chapter 3).

External effects also prevent the market from maximizing welfare. These effects happen when a good places costs or benefits on people not involved in its production or consumption. Pollution is an example of an external cost; protection from disease arising from another's immunization is an external benefit.

When there are external costs (see Chapter 5) the supply curve does not include all costs. The supply curve is the sum of marginal private (firms') costs ($S = \Sigma MPC$), but marginal social costs (MSC), which include external costs, are greater. Because costs, and so price, are lower than if all costs were borne internally, output is extended beyond the efficient level, and some units are produced which add more to social costs than to benefits.

Conversely, when there are external benefits (see Chapter 6), the demand curve does not reflect all societies' benefits from the consumption of a good, and there is under-production. Pure public goods may be regarded as an extreme case of external effects – all their benefits are external and they are not produced at all.

The failure of the market to provide incomes for all does not represent an efficiency failure. It is a failure to meet the distributional goal, however defined. There can be very different definitions of equity, but the fact that there are differences on how much redistribution there should be does not preclude agreement that some redistribution is necessary. The efficiency and equity problems that arise over redistribution are discussed in Chapter 8.

The newspaper cutting on page 18, 'Understanding how markets operate', contains the response of a reader – an economist – to a *Financial Times* leading article which showed little comprehension of how a market system operates. He explains the autonomous coordinating role of the market and points to the reality of market failure.

The mixed economy

In terms of resource allocation (*what? how?*), central planning fails fairly comprehensively. Markets are more successful, but they too misallocate resources and leave some people without incomes. A planned economy fails, but a market economy needs some planning. In the real world, economic systems are mixed.

Following the collapse of the eastern European and Soviet systems there seems to be some convergence for developed economies towards what is primarily a market system. The price mechanism allocates resources, but a government sector intervenes where the market fails.

Understanding how the markets operate

Sir, The Labour Party's new policy document declares that "the market can be a good servant, but is often a bad master." Your editorial comment ("Labour and the economy," May 21) disagrees. You assert that "a market is not an imposition upon the people; it is a name for exchange among them. If the market is a servant, so are the people – and the government is the master."

In these words you reveal not only a fundamental misunderstanding of how market economies actually operate, but also a woeful ignorance of the basic principles of economics.

A competitive market economy is not an aggregation of mutual contracts between people ("a name for exchange among them"), but an autonomous mechanism, operating outside the control of individual participants. As François Quesnay, the founder of modern economics, wrote in 1756, the market operates "independent of men's will."

That is why the subject of economics exists at all. Its role is to explain how that market mechanism actually works, how a myriad of individual decisions taken only in the light of market signals are coordinated by the invisible hand.

Proving the outcome to be efficient, even in some limited sense, requires mathematical assumptions too incredible to merit discussion – other than to point to the reality of market failure.

The elementary analysis of market failure suggests that, left to itself, the market will not ensure the socially desirable level of investment in education, in research, in infrastructure, or in the environment. In these cases the market is clearly a bad master.

And when next he is forced to modify his policies by the censure of the money markets, I am afraid that Mr Major will not be comforted by your belief that "if the market is a servant ... government is the master."

The FT should catch up with a modern understanding of what markets are about – or at least catch up with the economics of 1756.

John Eatwell,
Trinity College,
Cambridge

Financial Times, May 1990

Thus the public sector's function is to produce public goods, control monopoly, and change resource allocation by regulation and by taxes and subsidies where external effects lead to over- and under-production. It also ensures that people have minimum incomes.

Economies are also mixed in terms of their ownership systems. Internationally, within mixed though principally capitalist economies the spirit of the age has been towards privatization – less mixture, more capitalism (see *Privatization and the Public Sector* by Bryan Hurl). The formerly planned and socialist economies of eastern Europe (Poland, Hungary, etc.) are, at faster or slower rates, and with more or less success, moving both to markets and, via privatization, to capitalism. The states which constituted the USSR are following the same path. The problems of transition are enormous, and those who lived under the privations of planning probably had too rosy a view of what a market system can do, and of the merits of capitalism.

But in terms of the 'what to produce' and 'how to produce it' decisions the human mind has not been able to invent anything to match the market's ability to satisfy consumers' wants, and to do so efficiently. Provided that this fact does not blind us to its specific inefficiencies and to its inequities, we should join Adam Smith in admiration of the working of the 'invisible hand'. In the chapters that follow we discover where it gets things wrong and what can be done about it.

KEY WORDS

Economic system	Social costs
Market system	Social benefits
Command economy	Allocative efficiency
Capitalism	Productive efficiency
Socialism	Distributive efficiency
Perfect competition	Market failure
External effects	Mixed economy

Reading list

Healey, N., and Cook, M., Chapters 3 and 4 in *Supply side economics*, 3rd edn, Heinemann Educational, 1996.

Maunder, P., *et al.*, Chapter 2 in *Economics Explained*, 3rd edn, Collins Educational, 1995.

Essay topics

1. Explain what is meant by an optimum allocation of resources in a market economy. Why might an optimum allocation of resources *not* be achieved and what could or should the government do about this? [25 marks]
   [Northern Examinations and Assessment Board 1995]

2. (a) In a market economy, prices (i) give signals to participants in the economy; (ii) act as a rationing device; and (iii) provide incentives. Explain *each* of these functions. [12 marks]
   (b) Evaluate the economic arguments for and against introducing a system where schools charge their own fees and the government gives parents a voucher for each child which is used to contribute

towards school fees. [13 marks]
[Associated Examining Board 1995]

3. 'Not every government intervention in a market economy produces an increase in economic welfare.' Discuss. [25 marks]
[Oxford and Cambridge Schools Examination Board 1996]

4. 'Prices tell us what goods and services to produce and consume, and what employment to seek or offer.' – *Southern Africa Economist*, January 1991.
(a) Describe and explain the economic principles on which this statement is based. [12 marks]
(b) Is it best to leave the allocation of goods and labour to the price mechanism? [13 marks]
[University of Cambridge Local Examinations Syndicate 1995]

5. 'All economic agents (consumers, firms, government) have to choose, and that choice is limited.'
(a) Explain, in each case, why choices have to be made. [12 marks]
(b) In each case, how does the agent make choices? [13 marks]
[University of Oxford Delegacy of Local Examinations 1995]

Data Response Question

This task is based on a question set by the University of Cambridge Local Examinations Syndicate in 1996. Read the article opposite and then answer the questions.

1. With the aid of a diagram, explain the likely effect on the demand for the Space Shuttle of a fall in price charged by its competitors to launch a satellite. [5 marks]

2. (a) What is the difference between fixed costs and variable costs? [2 marks]
(b) Use the information provided in the table to allocate the costs of the Space Shuttle in terms of fixed and variable costs. Explain your answer. [3 marks]

3. (a) Explain why 'resources are most efficiently used when the price which is charged is equal to the marginal cost of providing one extra unit of the particular good or service'. [7 marks]
(b) Why is there a difference between the short-run marginal cost and the long-run marginal cost? [3 marks]

4. The US government wishes to carry out a cost–benefit analysis of the Space Shuttle programme. Outline the various costs and benefits it should consider and comment upon some of the problems it would have to overcome in carrying out this study. [20 marks]

The Space Shuttle

The Space Shuttle has been developed in the USA by the National Aeronautics and Space Administration (NASA). Its function is to put satellites into orbit for scientific, commercial and military purposes. It is not widely known that in carrying out this work, NASA applies market principles in order to determine the prices it should charge to its customers, both from the USA and elsewhere.

NASA operates in a competitive market. Its main competitors are Arianespace, operated by the European Space Agency, and a small number of private US firms. NASA estimates that, at a charge of $87m per flight, there would be an estimated demand of 24 flights per year for its services, with the competitors supplying the remainder of the market.

In determining prices, NASA has to take into account the prices charged by its main competitors who use traditional rockets which burn up in space. In contrast, the originality of the Space Shuttle is that it consists of an orbiter, which returns to earth and to which customers' rockets are attached. NASA operates four orbiters in its fleet and these can supply up to 25 flights in a year. The addition of a fifth orbiter would increase this capacity to 31 flights per year.

The table shows the estimated cost structure of NASA's operations. The capital charge item relates to the cost of the orbiter and the construction of the launch sites, whereas the flight costs are based on the costs incurred in putting the customers' rockets into space as required.

Estimated total and average costs for the Shuttle, fiscal years 1985–90 (million US$, 1982 prices)

	1985	1986	1987	1988	1989	1990
Capital charge	1803	1760	1707	1647	1586	1529
Flight programme costs	1782	1909	1985	2021	2013	2005
Total cost	3585	3669	3692	3668	3599	3534
Number of flights	11	16	21	23	24	24
Average total cost per flight	326	229	176	159	150	147

© *Pricing Options for the Space Shuttle,* reproduced by permission of the Congress of the United States, Congressional Budget Office, 1985

Economic theory advocates that resources are most efficiently used when the price charged is equal to the marginal cost of providing one extra unit of the particular good or service. This is the concept of allocative efficiency. In the case of the Space Shuttle, it has been estimated that the short-run marginal cost, using the four orbiters already constructed, is $42m per launch. If a further orbiter is constructed, the long-run marginal costs increase quite markedly to $75m per launch.

Chapter Three

Market failure and competition: theory

'" *You've no right to grow here,*" *said the Dormouse.*' Lewis Carroll

---

Markets can be characterized in terms of:

- the numbers of buyers and sellers, and
- the nature of the product that is bought and sold.

The efficiency of markets depends on the degree to which market prices reflect the costs of supply, on the one hand, and the preferences and satisfaction of the consumers on the other. For market prices to be sensitive to these influences, firms have to compete through price in both selling products and buying factors and be unable to dominate either other firms or consumers. The degree of price competition can, however, vary widely from zero to infinity.

In perfect **monopoly** a good is sold by a single seller and there are **barriers to entry** which prevent new firms from joining the industry to supply the market.

At the other extreme, **perfect competition** exists in markets where there are many firms all selling an identical, homogeneous product and where there is **freedom of entry** for new firms.

In each case the decision-makers do not have to bother about the effects of their decisions on other firms. In the first case there are none, and in the second case each firm is so small that, if it went out of business or doubled its output, it would have a negligible effect on market supply.

These two types of market structure define the extremes of a scale of price competition and are less commonly found in the real world. More common market structures comprise different numbers of firms of different sizes whose behaviour shows some degree of price competition but which also may have some of the characteristics of monopoly. The degree of **market power** is measured by the **concentration ratio**, which shows the percentage of sales held by the industry's largest firms. The four-firm or eight-firm concentration ratio is often cited. An example of considerable market power would be a 60 per cent four-firm concentration ratio.

An industry dominated by a few large firms whose behaviour is interdependent is an **oligopoly**. In oligopoly each firm has a significant share of total sales so that one firm's price and output decisions will affect the sales of its rivals. What it decides to do therefore depends on how it thinks its rivals will react; there is uncertainty. Profits would be higher if firms got together to agree to cut output and to raise price – that is, to reduce uncertainty by acting as if they were a monopoly. Thus **collusion** can take place, usually covertly because it is illegal, in order to fix price and output at levels to create extra monopoly profits.

The use of market power to distort prices and output from what they would have been under competitive equilibrium results in a reallocation of resources and a reduction in economic welfare. In what follows we shall evaluate the implications of competition and monopoly for the efficiency and equity of resource allocation. In the next chapter we review government policy toward monopoly.

Competition and efficiency

Figure 4 in Chapter 2 shows that allocative efficiency is achieved if output and price are set where the market demand and supply curves intersect. This is on the assumption that there are no externalities so that the supply curve represents all costs to society of producing the good (social cost); and that the consumers' benefits which give the demand curve represent all the benefits society obtains from consuming it (social benefit). For this ideal allocation to be achieved all markets in the economy must be perfectly competitive.

Under perfect competition, where there are large numbers of competing firms, the output of any one firm is such a small proportion of the total that any change in a single firm's output will have no effect on market price. This price is determined in the market for the good. Here the market supply curve is the sum of all firms' supply curves (which are their marginal cost curves) and the market demand curve is the sum of all consumers' demand curves (which are their marginal benefit curves). Price and output are set where market demand and supply curves intersect.

The situation is the same as that depicted in Figure 4 which shows **allocative efficiency**. If every industry and market were perfectly competitive (and if there were no external effects) then a market economy would achieve allocative efficiency.

Perfect competition also achieves **productive efficiency** – output at minimum resource cost. This requires that all firms produce at minimum average costs, and that all firms' costs are the same. We will now see how this happens. The competitive firm is a **price-taker** and the price set in the market gives each firm its demand curve. This is the

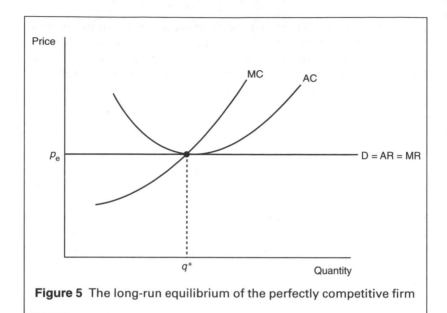

Figure 5 The long-run equilibrium of the perfectly competitive firm

perfectly elastic, horizontal, schedule at the ruling market price shown in Figure 5.

The perfectly elastic demand schedule shows that whatever quantity (up to the limit of its capacity) a firm puts on the market, the price is unaffected. If it attempted to get a higher price it would sell nothing, and as a **profit maximizer** it would not charge lower than the market price. The schedule shows the price at which all units may be sold – this is the average revenue obtained for each unit, and it is also the revenue received for each additional unit sold (marginal revenue). Hence we may label the curve: demand (D), average revenue (AR), and marginal revenue (MR). The firm's average and marginal cost curves (AC and MC) are also shown. **Normal profits**, the opportunity costs or returns necessary to keep resources producing this good rather than another, are included in the firm's costs.

The firm is in equilibrium when it maximizes profits, or minimizes losses. This happens when it produces every unit of output which adds more to revenue than to costs. This means that it will produce every unit up to that marginal one which costs as much to produce (MC) as it adds to revenue (MR). In Figure 5, q^* is the profit-maximizing output level, where MC = MR. To the left of q^*, MC < MR, so that units produced over this range add to the firm's profits; to the right of q^* each additional unit costs more to produce (MC) than it adds to revenue (MR); if any of these units were produced they would reduce the firm's profits. In Figure 5 it happens that at q^* where profits are maximized (MC = MR), average costs are at a minimum, and average costs equal average revenue – only normal profits are being made. We then need to ask if this is what we should expect to be the case. The answer is: in the short-run 'not necessarily', but in the long-run 'yes'.

In the short-run, price may be above the minimum average cost and above-normal profits will result. Output (where MC = MR = p) will be at a level above that which gives minimum average cost. But if this happens new firms will be attracted into the industry and price will be competed down until it is equal to average revenue and only normal profits are made. Thus, in the long-run, any profits above normal are competed away and high-cost firms go out of business, with the result that output is produced at minimum cost which is the same in all firms and maximum productive efficiency is achieved.

The firm's supply curve is its marginal cost curve. The marginal cost curve shows what quantity will be supplied at any price. The market supply curve is then the sum of the firms' supply or marginal cost curves (ΣMC). The market demand curve is the sum of the individual demand curves which show consumer benefits (ΣMB). Thus in perfect competition (and when there are no externalities), the supply curve shows the cost to society of each extra unit and the demand curve shows the benefits it provides. Output is at that point which maximizes welfare because only those units which provide more benefit than cost are produced, and firms are guided to produce at minimum cost. If this were the state of affairs over the whole of the economy, then there would be maximum output from the economy's resources, and maximum benefit to consumers from that output. Perfect competition would achieve Pareto efficiency (see Chapter 1).

Monopoly and efficiency

Under monopoly, which restricts output to achieve higher prices, some output which would add more to benefits than to costs is not produced. If we assume that costs are the same whether an industry operates under perfect competition or under monopoly (we will later drop this assumption), then monopoly output is lower and price is higher than under perfect competition. We assume the extreme monopoly case; a single firm producing all output. The firm *is* the industry and faces the downward-sloping market demand curve in Figure 6.

The schedule shows that the monopoly firm can set either price or

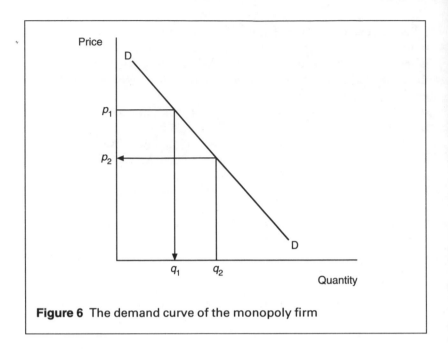

Figure 6 The demand curve of the monopoly firm

quantity but not both. If the firm sets the price for example at p_1, then the demand curve shows the quantity which will be bought, which is q_1. Or, if the firm puts a certain quantity on the market, then the price will be what the market will bear; for example if q_2 is offered for sale then the price must be p_2.

To increase sales the price must be reduced. It is not only the marginal buyer who will pay the lower price, but also those buyers already in the market who were paying the higher price. This means that when quantity sold is increased by a price reduction the addition to total revenue (marginal revenue) is not equal to the price (average revenue) obtained for that extra unit. This happens because some revenue is lost from intra-marginal buyers previously paying the higher price. For this reason marginal revenue lies below average revenue.

Pareto efficiency will not be achieved under monopoly. Figure 7 shows the demand curve facing the monopoly firm (D = AR) with its marginal revenue curve (MR) lying below, together with the average and marginal cost curves.

The monopoly firm which aims to maximize profits will produce all those units which add more to revenue than to cost. Up to *a* each unit provides the firm with more revenue than it costs to produce (MR > MC); beyond *a* each unit costs the firm more to produce than it adds to

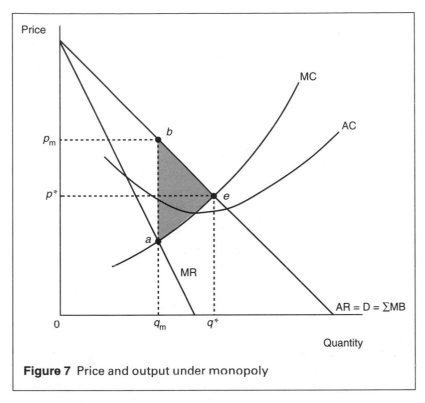

Figure 7 Price and output under monopoly

revenue (MC > MR). A profit-maximizing firm will therefore produce q_m, the quantity shown at a (where MC = MR); and the demand curve shows that q_m can be sold at price p_m.

This outcome is not allocatively efficient because resources are not allocated to produce some units of the good whose value to consumers is higher than their marginal cost of production. Pareto efficiency is not achieved. At q_m the marginal unit adds $q_m b$ to consumer welfare, but costs only $q_m a$ to produce. Units to the right of q_m are also valued more highly by consumers (shown by the demand curve) than they would cost to produce (MC curve). This is the case for each unit up to q^*, the optimal output where marginal costs and benefits are equal. The total loss of welfare arising from monopoly is the loss from not producing each potential unit of output between q and q^*. These would all add more to society's benefits than they would cost society to produce, but they remain unproduced because each one would involve the monopolist in a net loss of revenue.

The **deadweight loss** from monopoly is shown by the shaded area *abe*. It arises because resources are allocated *in*efficiently – they are not

27

used where there would be net welfare gains. If the monopoly were broken up into small units, the marginal cost curve (now the sum of many firms' marginal costs) would be the supply curve. Equilibrium would be at e where the demand and supply curves intersect. Price would be p^* and output would be at the efficient level, q^*.

Figure 7 shows that, as well as being allocatively inefficient, monopoly is also productively inefficient. At output q_m average costs are still falling because production is not at minimum average cost.

Monopoly and income distribution: consumer exploitation

As well as being inefficient, monopoly is inequitable. There is **consumer exploitation**. By restricting output and charging a higher price than in perfect competition, a firm with monopoly power extracts **monopoly profits**. It is likely that these profits go to well-off owners at the expense of less well-off consumers. It seems not unreasonable to regard redistribution of income by the rich to the rich as unfair.

In Figure 8, monopoly profits are shown as the difference, at output q_m, between total revenue $0p_mbq_m$ and total cost $0dcq_m$. They are represented by the shaded rectangle $dcbp_m$. As pure monopoly has been defined as a single firm supplying all output, with no competitors and with barriers to entry so that competitors are excluded, monopoly

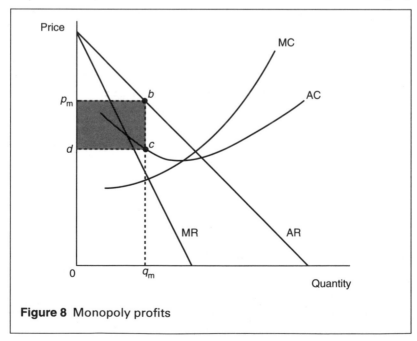

Figure 8 Monopoly profits

profits – above-normal, or super-normal, profits – will persist into the long-run.

Cartels

In the real world, monopolization of an industry by a single firm is far less likely than oligopoly. When competition is between a few firms it is in their interests, and it becomes possible for them, to collude to restrict output and to raise price in order to gain monopoly profits. When a group of firms overtly colludes on price and output it becomes a **cartel**.

More than 200 years ago Adam Smith warned of the propensity of businessmen to collude to raise their profits: 'People of the same trade seldom meet together, even for merriment and diversion, but the conversation ends in a conspiracy against the public or in some contrivance to raise prices' (*Wealth of Nations*). In most countries cartels are illegal. Collusion, which remains profitable, becomes covert.

Is monopoly always bad?

• Costs

The reasoning which showed that perfect competition produced a larger quantity at a lower price than did monopoly was based on the assumption that costs would be the same whether output was supplied by a large number of small firms or by a single seller. This assumption is unlikely to be the case in the real world. It is more probable that a monopolist would achieve economies of scale which would make costs lower than in perfect competition. If this is the case then monopoly, despite the restriction of output to raise price, and the consequent allocative inefficiency, might still provide a larger quantity at a lower price than perfect competition.

Figure 9 illustrates this. In the figure, p_c and q_c are competitive price and quantity, p_{m1} and q_{m1} are monopoly price and quantity with costs as in perfect competition, and p_{m2} and q_{m2} are monopoly price and quantity with reduced costs.

We must also note, however, that monopolies may incur *some* costs which do not arise in perfect competition. These are expenditures to maintain and reinforce their monopoly position – for example BT's advertising campaign to domestic consumers, 'It's good to talk' – and lobbying government for favourable treatment. Additionally it is argued that monopolies can have an 'easy life' because there are no competitive pressures on them to minimize costs. For example, it was claimed that British Gas did not 'drive hard bargains on the pay front'

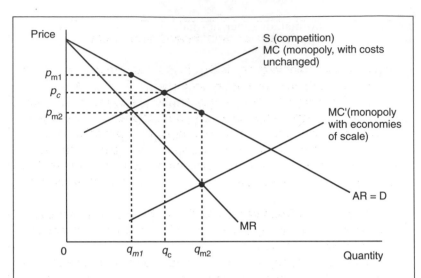

Figure 9 Lower costs in monopoly. p_c and q_c are competitive price and quality; p_{m2} and q_{m2} are monopoly price and quantity when there are economies of scale

(*Financial Times* leading article, 23 May 1991), nor do monopolies feel driven to obtain supplies at the lowest cost.

• Natural monopolies

'Natural monopolies' are an extreme case of the lower costs argument. A natural monopoly exists when average costs fall over a long range of output levels. If there are competing firms, the largest of the competitors will have the lowest costs and will force out the others. The larger it becomes (relative to the size of the market) the lower its average costs. Figure 10 in Chapter 4 depicts the natural monopoly.

Public utilities such as electricity supply, gas supply and water are all examples of natural monopolies. Overlapping local distribution systems would make no sense and would increase costs. In some natural monopolies, though not the utilities listed above, technological change makes competition possible. Telecommunications is an example.

• Invention, innovation and economic growth

The other principal argument in favour of monopoly is that in a capitalist market economy it promotes economic growth and that the **dynamic gains** to society from the **innovation** undertaken by monopolistic firms far outweigh **static losses** arising from misallocation. This

---

Capitalism, socialism and democracy

The essential point to grasp is that in dealing with capitalism we are dealing with an evolutionary process ...

Capitalism is by nature a form or method of economic change and not only never is but never can be stationary ... The fundamental impulse that sets and keeps the capitalist engine in motion comes from the new consumers' goods, the new methods of production or transportation, the new markets, the new forms of industrial organization that capitalist enterprise creates ...

This process of Creative Destruction is the essential fact about capitalism. It is what capitalism exists in and what every capitalist concern has got to live in.

... restrictive [monopolistic] practices ... acquire a new significance in the perennial gale of creative destruction, a significance which they would not have in a stationary state ...

... largest scale plans could in many cases not materialize at all if it were not known from the outset that competition will be discouraged by heavy capital requirements or lack of experience, or that means are available to discourage or checkmate it so as to gain the time and space for further developments ...

What we have got to accept is that [monopoly power] has come to be the most powerful engine of [economic] progress and in particular of the long-run expansion of total output not only in spite of, but to a considerable extent through, this strategy which looks so restrictive when viewed in the individual case and from the individual point of view ... It is hence a mistake to base the theory of government regulation of industry on the principle that big business should be made to work as the respective industry would work in perfect competition.

Adapted from Joseph A. Schumpeter, *Capitalism, Socialism and Democracy*, 4th edn, pp. 83–106, 1942

argument derives from a famous work, *Capitalism, Socialism and Democracy* (1942) by Joseph Schumpeter (see the extract above).

We have to ask whether Schumpeter's argument is correct. Does society gain more from the dynamic power of monopoly and oligopoly in promoting economic growth than it loses from the misallocation of resources?

The argument to support Schumpeter is that monopolies have both the ability, through high profits, and the incentive, through potential future profits which will not be competed away, to undertake the research and development which lead to new processes and new products. On the other hand, monopolists can survive even if they do not undertake these activities as they are insulated from competitive pressures. However, in most industries monopoly power is shared by a few large firms which makes them feel less secure than would a single monopoly firm, and so such behaviour less likely. Even where there is a single monopoly firm it is not sheltered forever because in the long-run substitutes can be found for nearly every good and service. Perhaps water is the only exception to this. For example, if gas became extremely expensive and inefficiently serviced, people would gradually turn to electricity to heat their homes and cook their food.

In contrast, it can be argued that the ability and motivation for competitive firms to innovate is much less. They do not have the monopoly profits to spend on research and development, and if they achieve technical advance and develop a new product or a new process, other firms are free to enter their market and share their rewards. To reap the benefits of innovation an innovating firm needs monopoly power. Governments give such monopoly power, for a certain period of time, by the granting of patents. A patent is a temporary legal monopoly and its intention is to stimulate innovation in competitive markets by enabling inventors to recoup the rewards of their genius, hard work and luck. It appears that for medium to large-sized firms, patent laws which protect profits from innovation are effective incentives to research and development.

Studies which have attempted to discover whether the dynamic gains from monopoly outweigh the deadweight loss show (for the USA) results varying from losses valued at 0.1 per cent to losses of 13 per cent of GNP – the latter also including costs directed at maintaining monopoly power. In the next chapter we turn to look at monopoly policy and the assumptions on which it is based. The USA, for example, starts with the assumption that monopoly power is always bad – 'You've no right to grow here', as Lewis Carroll's Dormouse said. But UK policy is more pragmatic, balancing costs against benefits.

KEY WORDS

Monopoly	Consumer exploitation
Barriers to entry	Monopoly profits
Perfect competition	Cartel
Freedom of entry	Economies of scale
Market power	Natural monopolies
Concentration ratio	Public utilities
Oligopoly	Dynamic gains
Collusion	Innovation
Allocative efficiency	Static losses
Productive efficiency	Research and development
Price-taker	New products
Profit-maximizer	New processes
Normal profits	Patents
Deadweight loss	

Reading list

Maunder, P., Chapter 22 in *Economics Explained*, 3rd edn, Collins Educational, 1995.

Stanlake, G. F., and Grant, S. J., Chapter 23 in *Introductory Economics*, 6th edn, Longman, 1995.

Essay topics

1. How and why is the structure of the market for national daily newspapers in the UK different from the structure of the world market for wheat? Discuss how the competitive behaviour of producers in these two markets is likely to differ. [25 marks]
   [Northern Examinations and Assessment Board 1995]
2. (a) With reference to different market structures, explain the factors which might prevent the entry of new firms into a market. [60 marks]
   (b) How might the existence of such barriers affect the profitability of a firm already operating in that market? [40 marks]
   [University of London Examinations and Assessment Council 1996]
3. (a) Explain, and illustrate with examples, how advertising and product differentiation can enable a firm to achieve monopoly power. [13 marks]
   (b) Discuss whether or not advertising and product differentiation are against the interest of consumers. [12 marks]
   [Associated Examining Board 1994]

4. 'Economies of scale result in large companies that dominate the market. Competition is thus reduced and, therefore, the exploitation of the consumer is inevitable.'
(a) Examine the economic issues raised in this argument. [15 marks]
(b) Discuss the extent to which you agree with it. [10 marks]
[University of Cambridge Local Examinations Syndicate 1996]

Data Response Question

This task is based on a question set by the University of Cambridge Local Examinations Syndicate in 1996. Read the information about Percy Engineering and then answer the questions below.

1. (a) To what extent can Percy Engineering be considered a monopolist? [3 marks]
(b) Describe briefly how the company originally gained its monopoly power in the UK market and how it may have subsequently retained it. [4 marks]
2. (a) Explain the term 'consumer surplus'. [2 marks]
(b) Use the figure to explain how consumer surplus changes if price rises from P_2 to P_1. [4 marks]
3. (a) From the figure identify the firm's total level of profits at the profit maximizing level of output if it charges the same price to all consumers. [2 marks]
(b) Explain how Percy Engineering would not maximize profits if it produced output Q_2. [3 marks]
(c) Explain why Percy Engineering might use price discrimination as a way of further increasing the overall profitability of its business. [6 marks]
4. Why might Percy Engineering not always maximize profits? [8 points]
5. (a) What evidence would you collect in order to report to the government on whether Percy Engineering is currently acting against the public interest? [8 marks]
(b) Discuss the action that the government might take if Percy Engineering were found to be acting against the public interest. [10 marks]

Percy Engineering

Percy Engineering is the only manufacturer in the UK of the 'Snow Pusher', a specialist type of snow-moving equipment which is attached to the front of a lorry. It was patented by its inventor and owner in 1954. The company supplies 80 per cent of all such devices used by local authorities and private contractors in the UK.

Most economists would be concerned about the behaviour of firms such as Percy Engineering which have a very large share of a particular market. It is felt that their monopoly power often allows them to restrict output, raise prices and determine their own scale of production, so enhancing company profits at the expense of the consumer. The figure shows the overall marginal and average revenue curves (MR and AR) which the firm believes it is currently facing, along with its short-run marginal and average total cost curves (MC and ATC).

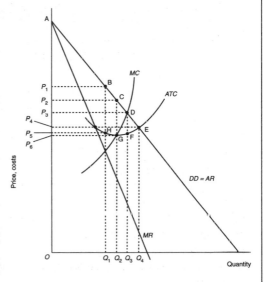

Percy Engineering has been successful in exporting Snow Pushers to the rest of the European Union (EU), its exports reaching a peak in 1990/91 when they accounted for about half the total revenue of the business. Most recently, the company has lost some of its market share to lower cost producers from South East Asia, who have been particularly successful in producing a similar product for the European market.

Consequently, Percy Engineering has made losses from its business in the rest of the EU and these have had to be funded from profits earned in the UK domestic market. The firm's market share in the UK has held up well in spite of its difficulties in the rest of the EU. However, recent research by an independent group of economists has estimated that the price elasticity of demand for Snow Pushers in the UK market is less than in the rest of the EU. This has prompted Percy Engineering to review its pricing policy, which currently involves charging the same price for Snow Pushers in all of its markets.

Chapter Four
Competition policy

'"In that case," said the Dodo, "I move that the meeting adjourn, for the immediate adoption of more energetic remedies."' Lewis Carroll

A pure monopoly, where consumers have no alternative supplier or product, can be inefficient, ill-serve its consumers and still make high profits. The extract 'Drought area's big water profit' illustrates this.

Drought area's big water profit

Yorkshire Water yesterday came under fire for earning record profits while offering its customers a sub-standard service. The company, which has a hosepipe ban in force after water shortages last year, reported 1995/96 pre-tax profits of £162.2 million. This was more than £20 million above the previous year despite £47 million spent on a round-the-clock tanker operation to bring water to drought-hit West Yorkshire last summer.

Consumer groups and politicians were outraged that the company had been increasing profits while customers were suffering because of failures by the company. Two recent reports, one by an independent expert commissioned by the board and the other by Ofwat, the industry regulator, criticised the company's management for failing to anticipate demand and to check leaks. ...

There was anger in Halifax. "It is appalling," said Maureen Richards, a civil servant from nearby Brighouse. She said that instead of forcing her family to recycle its bath water, the company ought to recycle its profits into improving supplies.

The Guardian, 6 June 1996

Earlier in the 1990s it was pointed out how persistent are monopoly profits. In 1991–92, a year of deep recession, privatized utilities' dividends grew by an average 10 per cent, which compared with an average increase of only 1 per cent for other, all-share, dividends. A commentor wrote:

> *'The worry is that the creation of a profit conscious utility sector, ready to exploit its monopoly position for commercial gain, is doing serious harm to the competitiveness of the rest of the economy* [which had to pay higher prices for power and water than its overseas competitors]'

Barry Riley, *Financial Times*, June 1992

Since that time the various **regulators** of the electricity, gas and water industries – OFFER, OFGAS, OFWAT – have been through a learning process and are becoming more assiduous in their defence of the consumer, but the problem has not gone away.

The problem of monopoly profits and consumer exploitation arises not only from single-firm monopolies like the **privatized utilities,** but also from cartels where firms band together in order to extract monopoly profits. Governments must have policy measures and authorities to police and control monopoly power wherever it appears.

"It's not a telephone – it's a profit maximisation module"

Competition policy

In their competition policy governments seek efficiency and equity. Policies aim at minimizing the misallocation of resources caused by monopoly, and at preventing the exploitation of consumers. There are broadly two possible approaches:

- the first seeks to break up monopoly and to make it more like competitive industry;
- the second aims not to break up but to regulate it with permanent bodies to investigate and to oversee potential abusers of monopoly power.

The first approach has long been used in the USA, the second repre sents the British way. The American approach would appear to be based on the presumption that monopoly is necessarily bad, whereas the British attitude is more pragmatic – it judges each case on its merits and balances the gains from monopoly against the costs:

- economies of scale
- strength in international competition
- the efficiency of the particular firm
- research and development
- long-run growth

are set against:

- output restriction
- consumer exploitation
- lack of incentive to minimize costs.

On this basis the **Monopolies and Mergers Commission (MMC)** investigates cases referred to it by the **Office of Fair Trading (OFT)** which supervises competition and consumer law. However, British policy against cartels can, in practice, be extremely feeble (see the extract on page 41 entitled 'Monopolies and mergers omission'). British companies may also be caught by EU law, which is potentially more severe even than US law, but it applies only to international trade.

Policy and natural monopolies: nationalization, privatization and regulation

Figure 10 shows a natural monopoly, such as electricity distribution, where larger output leads to lower average costs. Over the whole range of output, marginal cost lies below average cost.

Without regulation, equilibrium is at e where MC = MR. This leads to price p_m at output q_m and monopoly profits are made. This compares with the allocatively efficient output and price at p^* and q^* where MC = MB (given by the average revenue curve). At this output, price/average revenue (set equal to marginal cost) is below average cost so that losses are made.

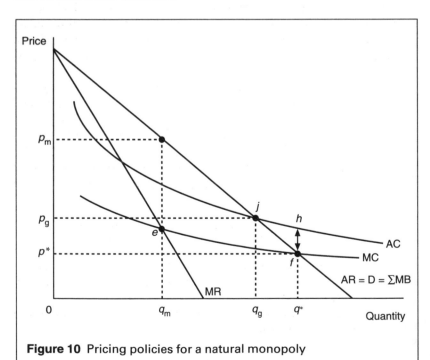

Figure 10 Pricing policies for a natural monopoly

To reduce or remove misallocation and exploitation of the consumer, public policy aims to increase output and reduce price. For Pareto efficiency, output should be at q^* with price p^*. The average loss, fh per unit sold, would be covered by a subsidy of fh per unit whether the firm were in the private or public sector. However, this outcome represents the ideal, or first-best, efficiency. It would be the outcome sought if everywhere in the economy price were set equal to marginal cost.

However, if in most of the rest of the economy perfect competition does not prevail then a second-best solution might be recommended: output at j where average cost and average revenue are equal, with output q_g and price p_g .The principle of the second best means that if in the rest of the economy the first best outcome (MSC = MSB) does not hold then it is inefficient to enforce that outcome in a single sector. Though j is not the first-best solution, output q_g is larger than in monopoly, monopoly profits are eliminated, and as revenues cover costs, this is achieved without the imposition of an additional tax burden on the economy to pay for the subsidy which would be necessary if price were equal to marginal cost.

The state can aim at achieving its preferred outcome either by taking natural monopolies into public ownership (**nationalization**) or by regulation. Both have been tried in the UK. From the late 1940s to the mid-eighties public utilities were publicly owned, whereas in the eighties they were privatized. During the time when many public utilities were in public ownership, average-cost pricing was preferred to marginal-cost pricing. MC pricing leads to losses that have to be financed by taxation, which can cause distortions elsewhere. Additionally the expectation of losses means the absence of pressure on managers to minimize costs.

In the 1980s many publicly owned monopolies, including natural monopolies, were privatized. The **privatization** programme focused attention on two issues:

- whether monopolies should be in the public or private sector;
- whether policy should aim at competition or regulation.

The two issues are interconnected: the answer to the second (is competition possible?) will affect the answer to the first (is privatization desirable?). The undoctrinaire will approve of privatization for industries where competition is feasible, but will prefer true monopolies to remain in public ownership.

Recent UK competition policy

For some privatized public utilities competition is feasible, for example in telecommunication and electricity generation. But natural monopolies, where competition is not feasible, persist: electricity distribution to small consumers and water supply within a single area. Even where there has been break-up the drive to combine still persists (see the electricity industry experience below). In these circumstances regulation and associated authorities must exist to protect consumers.

The privatized utilities were each provided with their own regulators – OFTEL, OFFER, OFGAS, OFWAT – for telecommunications, electricity, gas and water, respectively. The principal means of regulation has been a formula for price increases, '**RPI minus** x', where the x per cent deducted from the Retail Prices Index is set to take account of the potential for efficiency gains. (The water companies are more generously treated – price increases are permitted to provide funds for investment.)

The regulators' activity and success has varied, but experience and time has improved it. A serious problem remains for successful regulation – access to all the necessary information on which to base decisions. Industries which have more knowledge than their regulators may outsmart and outmanoeuvre them.

There is a fairly general view that UK competition policy is in a mess. In particular the Monopolies and Mergers Commission is criticized. For several years proposals for reform have been mooted, but no change has been undertaken. In 1989 Mrs Thatcher's government published a White Paper setting out proposals to reform the 1976 Restrictive Practices Act, but nothing was done. In 1992 there followed a Green Paper (Green Papers normally precede White Papers), but nothing developed. In March 1996 there was a Consultation Document.

The debate came to a head in April 1996 when the MMC recommended that the two electricity generators, PowerGen and National Power, should be permitted to take over two regional electricity distribution companies, Midlands Electric and Southern Electric, respectively. Privatization had separated generation from distribution in order to encourage competition by letting regional electricity firms shop around for the lowest price from the generators, and to provide a market for new entrants to the generation industry. It was argued that integration of the regional distribution monopolies with the large generators would undermine this: generators would sell to captive distribution companies with captive customers. So:

- what little competition there is in electricity would be reduced;
- new entrants would be deterred;
- vertical integration would make the industry even more opaque and difficult to regulate;
- prices to consumers would rise.

The MMC recommended, however, that the takeovers be permitted. The rationale for this recommendation was that strong companies ('national champions') with large shares of the domestic market would be able to compete abroad, partly through increased size and partly because of a wider range of skills and experience. The MMC thought this was more important than the protection of the consumer.

Monopolies and Mergers Omission

.... the government's failure to reform Britain's competition laws has damaged competitiveness. Lord Borrie, director-general of fair trading from 1976 to 1992, complained last year that current policy was distinguished by 'lack of will, dither and uncertainty'.

A series of recent MMC reports have dismissed complaints about restraints to competition in markets ranging from instant coffee and ice-cream to perfume and cars. Even where the MMC has decided to act, its proposed remedies have sometimes been so weak, notably on newspaper distribution and gas supplies, that they have had to be toughened by the Office of Fair Trading, the MMC's sister body, which in theory is supposed to carry out initial investigations while the MMC does the in-depth work. The weakness of government competition policy may spring partly from concerns about whether or not tough anti-monopoly legislation is good for an economy; but it has manifested itself as dithering. ...

Mr Odgers (the MMC's chairman), a former managing director of Tarmac, argued on taking office (1993) that overzealous enforcement of competition rules 'risked damaging our great enterprises'. It was vital, he added, that the interests of industry were properly looked after: 'Competition can be enormously beneficial in many cases, but where it involves the destruction of strong interests in a wider context, it could be weakening from UK plc's point of view.'...

Complaints about the MMC are only part of a wider criticism about the ineffectiveness and confusion of Britain's competition laws. The overlapping jurisdiction between the OFT and the MMC causes concern. The present set-up's most influential critic is Sir Bryan Carsberg, who resigned as director-general of fair trading last year because he was so frustrated by the government's failure to reform competition laws. He argues that a single regulatory body would be more effective than the current confusion of laws and responsibilities. If Labour wins the next election and fulfils its manifesto commitments, he may well get his way.

The Economist, 20 April 1996

There was a storm of protest, and Ian Lang, Trade and Industry Secretary, in 'one of the momentous events in the history of UK competition policy' (*Financial Times*) blocked the takeover.

In the view of the *FT* and other serious commentators this cast the role and competence of the MMC into question. The March 1996 consultation paper had already put forward ideas for an overhaul of the UK's competition policy and authorities. It seems likely that there will be reform; the extract 'Monopoly and mergers omission' from *The Economist* argues for change.

The motivation and ability of companies to make monopoly profits is an object lesson to students of economics. More energetic remedies, as the Dodo remarked, are needed.

KEY WORDS

Regulators	Office of Fair Trading
Privatized utilities	Nationalization
Monopolies and Mergers Commission	Privatization
Commission	RPI minus x

Reading list

Hurl, B., *Privatization and the Public Sector*, 3rd edn, Heinemann Educational, 1995.

Maunder, P., *et al.*, Chapter 27 in *Economics Explained*, 3rd edn, Collins Educational, 1995.

Essay topics

1. (a) Explain how in economic theory a monopolist determines price and output. [10 marks]

   (b) Privatization of the UK water supply industry created a number of regional monopolies. Discuss whether it is better for water to be supplied by the private sector rather than the public sector. [15 marks]

   [University of Cambridge Local Examinations Syndicate 1995]

2. (a) Explain briefly the meaning of the terms 'barriers to entry' and 'barriers to exit'. [30 marks]

   (b) How might barriers to entry be expected to affect the way in which markets operate in the real world? Illustrate your answer with relevant examples. [70 marks]

   [University of London Examinations and Assessment Council 1996]

3. 'The prospects for consumers of gas and electricity have never been better.' Discuss. [25 marks]
   [Oxford and Cambridge Schools Examination Board 1996]
4. Examine the economic justifications for, and activities of, *two* of the following: (a) the Monopolies and Mergers Commission; (b) OFWAT (the water industry Official Regulator); (c) the National Health Service; (d) the Bank of England. [25 marks]
   [University of Oxford Delegacy of Local Examinations 1995]

Data Response Question

This task is based on a question set by the University of London Examinations and Assessment Council in 1996. Study Tables A and B and then answer the questions that follow.

Table A National newspaper circulations in the UK

| Title of newspaper | Owned by | Daily circulation | | |
		1992	1993	1994
Sun	News Corporation	3 588 077	3 513 591	4 007 520
Daily Mirror	Headington Investment	2 868 263	2 676 015	2 484 436
Daily Mail	Daily Mail	1 688 808	1 769 253	1 784 030
Daily Express	United Newspapers	1 537 726	1 490 323	1 369 266
Daily Telegraph	Ravelston Corporation	1 043 703	1 024 340	1 007 944
Daily Star	United Newspapers	808 486	773 908	746 412
Today	News Corporation	495 405	533 332	579 910
Guardian	Guardian Newspapers	418 026	416 207	400 300
Times	News Corporation	390 323	368 219	471 847
Independent	Newspaper Publishing	376 532	348 692	284 440
Financial Times	Pearson	291 915	290 139	296 984
		13 507 264	13 204 019	13 433 188

Table B UK newspaper price reductions in early 1993

	Old price	New price
Sun	25 p	20 p
Times	45 p	20 p
Daily Telegraph	48 p	30 p

1. With reference to Table A, comment on the view that News Corporation was a monopoly in the market for national daily newspapers in 1994. [3 marks]
2. Suggest *two* reasons why some newspaper companies publish more than one newspaper title. [4 marks]
3. Some of the other newspaper publishers considered that the price reductions announced by News Corporation for the *Sun* and the *Times* were an example of predatory pricing. (a) Explain what is meant by 'predatory pricing'; and (b) examine *three* reasons which might explain why News Corporation embarked on such a pricing policy. [3, 6 marks]
4. To what extent might newspaper publishing be regarded as a contestable market? [5 marks]
5. In the UK, newspaper publishers are prevented from controlling domestic independent television companies. Why might newspaper publishers seek to expand into other media? [4 marks]

Chapter Five

Externalities 1: external costs

' *"That's right, Five! Always lay the blame on others!"* ' Lewis Carroll

What are externalities

The **external effects** of economic activities are an important reason for markets failing to provide an efficient allocation of resources. Externalities happen when costs are imposed on, or when benefits are given to, firms or households who are not parties to the transactions which have these effects. Externalities are by-products or side-effects of production or consumption or both.

- **External costs** are found, for example, in social, economic and environmental problems such as slum housing, traffic congestion, pollution and the depletion of the ozone layer.
- **External benefits** arise, for example, from public transport, well-maintained housing, education and health care.

If a factory emits pollutants into the air, local households have to spend money on detergents and time on cleaning which would not otherwise be necessary, and some people may become ill because of the polluted atmosphere. These are part of the polluting firm's production costs, but they are imposed on third parties and are not borne by the firm, and they are not charged in the price to the consumers of its products. The consequence of under-pricing is **over-production**.

If, on the other hand, public transport makes for less traffic congestion and pollution then car drivers and local inhabitants are the third parties who gain external benefits. However, again, these benefits are external to the market and do not affect prices. The consequence is **under-production** – a lower level of output than would happen if all benefits were reflected in the price.

Thus, there is a *misallocation of resources* to the production of goods which have external effects, and the outcome is not allocatively efficient. Equity, too, is not achieved because costs are imposed on third parties who receive no compensation, and benefits are gained by people who make no payment.

This chapter is about external costs. It shows how over-production comes about and discusses the policies necessary to achieve the optimal level of output and hence an efficient allocation of resources.

Chapter 6 is about external benefits, their causes and consequences and how allocative efficiency can be attained where they exist.

External costs

One of the instances in the previous section, air pollution inflicted on neighbouring households by a local firm, is an example of a *producer-to-consumer* externality.

'One, two, three, four, five, once I caught a fish alive'

A classic example of a *producer-to-producer* external cost is the pollution of river water by an upstream firm when clean water is required by a downstream firm. If the downstream firm has to install equipment to clean the polluted water before it can be used, this is a production cost of the first firm imposed on the second.

Alcohol consumption is an activity which causes both *consumer-to-consumer* and *consumer-to-producer* external costs. It causes road accidents and fights which result in hospital bills that are borne by individuals and society; and it impairs workers' efficiency and their health and thereby imposes costs on their employers.

Externalities and the environment

The examples of external costs given so far, though very serious for those who bear them, are all relatively small scale when compared with worldwide environmental problems.

Acid rain, which crosses national boundaries and arises from sulphur dioxide emissions from coal-fired power stations and nitrogen oxide from vehicles, has long been a problem. More recently concern has grown for the large-scale external costs which can be imposed on the whole planet and on future generations. These are the well-known problems of **global warming** caused by the emission of carbon dioxide (CO_2) and other greenhouse gases and **ozone depletion** by chlorofluorocarbons

(CFCs). They are costs of production and consumption imposed principally by developed economies on all their own citizens, and on the less developed world, and potentially on future generations.

Global warming will raise sea levels and may destroy some of the places where people live and work; it will change climate patterns and change food production. Destruction of the ozone layer which protects us from ultraviolet radiation can lead to skin cancers and corneal cataracts. Whether traditional economic analysis and policies based on it are appropriate when the future of the planet may be at stake is a matter of debate and will be discussed in the final section.

External costs: inefficient and unfair

External costs are both inefficient and unfair. Because the producer does not bear all costs and pass them on to the consumer in price, output is extended beyond the allocatively efficient quantity where MSC = MSB. Some units are produced for which social costs exceed social benefits. The inequity arises because third parties have costs imposed on them for which they receive no compensation.

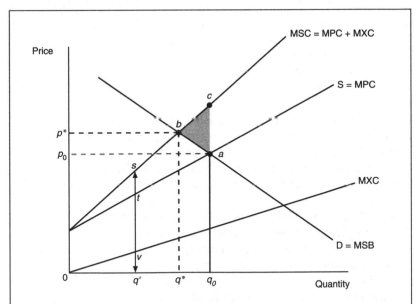

Figure 11 External costs and misallocation; output too high and price too low. The market outcome, at *a* where S = D, under-prices (p_0) and over-provides (q_0). Optimal output, q^*, is at *b* where marginal social benefit (MSB) = marginal social cost (MSC)

Figure 11 shows how allocative inefficiency arises. There is over-production because the supply curve does not take account of all production costs. The demand curve (D) is the marginal social benefit schedule (MSB) on the assumption that there are no external benefits from consumption. The supply curve (S) is the sum of firms' marginal cost curves, which are **marginal private costs** (MPCs) only. However, the production of this good imposes external costs such as air or water pollution, and these rise as output rises; they are shown by the **marginal external cost** (MXC) curve.

Social costs include both private and external costs. They are shown in the diagram by the **marginal social cost** (MSC) schedule which is obtained when the marginal external cost of each unit is added to the marginal private cost of the unit. The MSC schedule is the vertical sum of MPC and MXC. For example, the unit q' costs society $q's$, made up of $q't$, the private cost, plus $q'v$ (= ts), the external cost.

The optimum level of output is q^*, where MSC = MSB, but the private market extends production to q_0, where D = S. But for each unit between q^* and q_0 MSC is greater than MSB, so these units should not be produced. The **deadweight loss** from their production is the excess of social cost over social benefit for each unit – zero for the unit q^*, up to ac for the unit at q_0, the total amount being given by the triangle abc.

We should note that at q^* external costs will happen – pollution (if this is the cost) is not eliminated; in this example only at output zero are there no external costs. However, for each unit between zero and q^* marginal social benefit is greater than the marginal social cost; that is, benefits are greater than the sum of both private and external costs. Therefore it is efficient for each of these units to be produced. The efficient level of pollution, the **optimal externality**, is obtained.

Finally we should note that it is easy to draw a diagram showing external costs precisely, and a precisely quantifiable output which would bring about optimal allocation. In practice, however, estimation of external costs is extremely difficult. Nevertheless a diagrammatic approach is of value because it gives a clear representation of what the problem is.

Property rights and externalities

External costs arise because people have no **property rights** in the good which is used or depleted by those imposing these costs. For example, inhabitants of a neighbourhood do not own the air that surrounds them so they cannot charge the polluting factory for using it as a dump for waste products. The downstream factory does not own the river water and so cannot charge the upstream firm for discharging chemicals into it.

If the air and water *were* owned by these third parties they could charge the polluters for their use of them. This would *internalize the externality*, and all costs would be borne by the producer. The supply curve, private costs, would include what previously were external costs, and would represent social costs. Price would be higher and an efficient allocation of resources – production at q^* in Figure 11 – would be achieved. This solution would also be fair because those whose air or water became dirtier would receive monetary compensation for the costs they had to bear. The **'polluter-pays' principle** would be achieved.

Even if property rights over the air and water were held by the polluting factories, an efficient solution could be achieved as the sufferer could pay, or 'bribe', the polluters to cut back on pollution. This could happen because between q^* and q_0 external costs are greater than private gains to the polluter so that the sufferers could compensate the polluter and still be better off than with the excess pollution. This, though efficient, would not be a fair outcome because it would be the sufferers, not the polluter, who paid for pollution abatement.

What can governments do?

Policy to control pollution and other external costs can take two forms: **regulatory controls** or **market methods**, including **taxation** and **tradeable pollution permits**.

Regulations are legal requirements to comply with physical standards and they have had some success in the UK in cleaning our air and rivers. Taxation and permits, on the other hand, operate through the price mechanism. In most cases economists prefer market methods as they are more efficient than laws. Refer to the extract 'Environmental economic policy' on page 50.

Figure 12 shows how taxation can correct the resource misallocation caused by external costs. Like Figure 11 it shows a demand curve (D = MSB) and a supply curve (S = MPC), together with marginal external costs which added to the supply curve give marginal social costs. In addition, tax policy shows how the externality/pollution can be reduced.

A policy to cut output from q_0 to q^* is needed: price must rise. The supply curve needs to be shifted up so that the supply price includes the external cost. The amount by which it needs to be shifted up is the amount of marginal external cost at q^*, which is $q^*e = db$. A unit tax t equal to db shifts the supply curve up to the broken line: supply curve

Environmental economic policy

The groundwork has now been laid for a different kind of environmental policy based on changing *economic incentives*.

Traditional 'command and control' regulations can be used to drive a wedge between economic activity and its environmental impact. A flue gas desulphurization plant, for example, leaves the amount of coal-fired electricity largely unaffected but 'takes the sulphur out' from the chimney stack. Economic activity (electricity production) has then been decoupled from environmental impact (acid rain).

But there are far more efficient ways of achieving the same thing. The sulphur content of coal could be taxed. The power station then has a choice of how to react. If it reduces sulphur emissions it pays less tax. It may do this by investing in a desulphurization plant, or seeking efficiency improvements, or using lower sulphur coal, or even by switching to another fuel entirely.

The tax gives the producer *flexibility* in response and this will lead to the cheapest technology being used. Environmental quality does not suffer, but compared with the command and control approach compliance costs are lower. This is important in a world where environmental regulations daily get tougher, not laxer.

An alternative flexible instrument for controlling pollution is the *tradeable permit*. Instead of taxing the sulphur emissions we could place a 'bubble' over the power generation sector such that the sector as a whole cannot emit more than a certain level of emissions. Within the bubble, however, the industry is free to increase emissions so long as there is an equivalent reduction elsewhere. An efficient procedure is to allow the credits to be traded. We might control vehicle pollution this way as well. Vehicle manufacturers could be given 'miles per gallon' quotas. If they produced cars that did better than the quota, they could sell the resulting credit to other manufacturers. Again, the process is flexible.

The critical features of this economic approach are that:

- it is very likely to cost significantly less than the traditional regulatory approach (US studies suggest savings in compliance costs of at least half);
- it gives flexibility to polluters;
- it secures the same environmental quality objectives as the traditional approach;
- it stimulates clean technology.

Adapted from 'Toward the sustainable economy: environment and economics' by David Pearce, *Royal Bank of Scotland Review*, December 1991

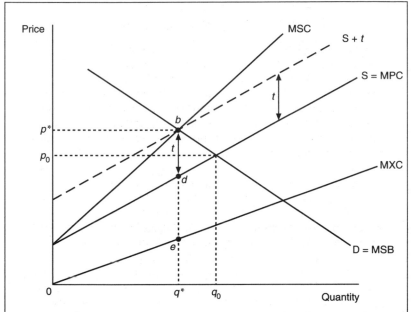

Figure 12 Taxation to reduce an external cost. A unit tax, *t*, raises prices so that quantity is cut from q_0 to q^*, the optimal amount

$S + t$. Thus the tax raises price to p^* and cuts output to the allocatively efficient level, q^*. External costs still arise, pollution is not eliminated but it is now an optimal externality. *Claiming, as here, that efficiency has been achieved assumes away all the problems of measuring external costs and getting the tax at the right level. In practice these problems are very difficult and very important.*

Efficiency is, in theory, achievable; equity, however, is more problematical. Those who benefit from the good whose production or consumption causes the externality (say pollution) and those who suffer are probably different groups. For example the polluters, who gain benefits, may be car-driving commuters from the suburbs and the sufferers may be those who live near inner-city ring roads and interchanges. The tax paid by the polluters when they buy petrol does not go in compensation to those sufferers, but to the government. If the inner-city dwellers had property rights in the air around them they could have charged commuters for its use. But this solution is possible only in theory; the large numbers which would be involved on both sides of the bargaining process make it unworkable in practice.

Policy for the planet and the future

Finally we should look at the problems listed earlier which may threaten the future of life on earth: global warming and ozone depletion. There have been two debates on these problems. The first debate was in two parts: (a) whether or not they existed, and (b) if they did exist whether they were a matter of concern. The second debate, accepting their existence, was on what should be done about them.

On the first debate there was a minority view that we should not be worried by the environmentalists and their alarmist stories. This opinion is encapsulated in the writing of Russell Lewis, one-time Director of the Conservative Political Centre. His article in *Economic Affairs*, journal of the right-wing think tank the Institute of Economic Affairs, included the following thoughts:

- The greens are in retreat ... but green scares persist.
- A warmer earth might be nicer.
- An ozone hole may only be seasonal.
- Global warming may not be harmful – ultraviolet rays are decreasing.
- Ecology needs the market approach.

However, governments have now accepted conclusive results from meteorologists and environmental scientists that the problems exist, and that they should be taken very seriously.

The last of Lewis's points ('Ecology needs the market approach') takes us on to the second debate. Given that global warming and ozone depletion exist and that something needs to be done, what form should policy take? For smaller-scale problems it was suggested in the previous section that a market-led approach was more efficient than regulations and laws, and so more likely to result in an optimal outcome. However, the optimal outcome includes the optimal quantity of pollution, the optimal externality. Where the externality may be the destruction of the protective ozone layer, the costs may be unquantifiably large and imposed on future generations, so there may be no optimal quantity of pollution. A market approach, which might permit the continued production of CFCs, would not achieve the desired solution. Regulations, physical controls (for example a ban on CFC production) are needed.

However, even for the big problems market methods do have a part to play. A favoured method to limit CO_2 emissions is **carbon taxes** which would make the use of fossil fuels and other contributors to greenhouse gases more expensive. This would lead to greater economy in their use, would motivate people to insulate their homes, and would stimulate the development of alternative power sources (for example solar energy) which are at present uneconomic.

External costs vary from the trivial (next-door's bonfire) to the catastrophic (Chernobyl); they affect the present and the future. What this chapter has tried to show is how economic analysis can lead to an understanding of what they are, how they arise, the inefficiency and inequity they cause, and how public policy can deal with them. The aim of policy is to prevent polluters from behaving like Lewis Carroll's character, Five, always laying the blame on others. However, we have found that there may be limits to economic solutions.

KEY WORDS

External effects	Marginal social cost
Externalities	Deadweight loss
External costs	Optimal externality
External benefits	Property rights
Over-production	'Polluter-pays' principle
Under-production	Regulatory controls
Acid rain	Market methods
Global warming	Taxation
Ozone depletion	Tradeable pollution permits
Marginal private cost	Carbon taxes
Marginal external cost	

Reading list

Burningham, D., and Davies, J., Chapters 1, 2, 3 and 6 in *Green Economics*, Heinemann Educational, 1995.

Essay topics

1. Atmospheric pollution is often described as a 'negative externality'. Explain what is meant by this. To what extent is the reduction of pollution in the UK possible through the operations of the market? [20 marks]
   [Northern Examinations and Assessment Board, AS level, 1996]

2. (a) Explain why environmental pollution is regarded as a source of market failure. [12 marks]
   (b) Evaluate *two* different policies which a government might implement to reduce pollution. [13 marks]
   [Associated Examining Board 1996]

3. In September 1994 a report by the Royal Commission on Environmental Pollution recommended that the price of petrol should be doubled and government expenditure on public transport should be substantially increased. Analyse (a) the case for and (b) the likely economic effects of implementing these proposals. [40, 60 marks]
   [University of London Examinations and Assessment Council 1996]

4. A chemical company is known to discharge effluent into the local river.
   (a) Using a diagram, explain why this is indicative of market failure. [10 marks]
   (b) A local environmental group wants to close the company down. An economist suggests indirect taxation to deal with this problem of perceived market failure. Assess the relative merits of these two policies as a means of improving resource allocation. [15 marks]
   [University of Cambridge Local Examinations Syndicate 1996]

Data Response Question

This task is based on a question set by the Associated Examining Board in 1994. Study the passage below which is adapted from 'A market made out of muck' by Barbara Durr, published in the *Financial Times*, 10 June 1992. Answer the questions that follow.

The passage describes a scheme introduced in the USA which aims to reduce the pollution caused by coal-burning power stations. The scheme is based on setting, and then each year gradually reducing, maximum limits or ceilings for pollution. Under the scheme a power station which 'over-complies' – i.e. one that cuts pollution by more than is required – is allowed to sell its spare pollution allowances. The allowance, or 'permit to pollute', can be bought by an 'under-complying' power station – one that has cut pollution by less than is required. Note that one allowance equals one tonne of sulphur dioxide.

A market in 'permits to pollute'

Last month, three US utility companies bravely waded into a national experiment to use market principles for environmental ends and to tackle a problem of 'market failure'. In the first public deal to trade 'permits to pollute', the Wisconsin Power & Light Company sold 10 000 allowances to the Tennessee Valley Authority and between 15 000 to 25 000 allowances to the Duquesne Light Company in Pittsburgh.

The allowances are part of the Clean Air Act of 1990, which requires America's mostly coal-burning utilities to halve their emissions of sulphur dioxide, the key

---

ingredient in acid rain, by the year 2000. The national cap on sulphur dioxide emissions will be achieved in the most economically efficient way by trading the rights to pollute among utilities. Under the Act, those companies which exceed compliance with the emissions standard – by installing new cleaner technology or switching to lower sulphur fuels – can sell their spare allowances, issued by the Environmental Protection Agency (EPA), to those who have not fully complied.

The electricity market is a 'regulatory-driven market'. As yet however, the public utility commissions that regulate the American private power companies have not spelled out who – the consumers of electricity or the companies' shareholders – are to benefit (or lose) from the effects on electricity prices and company costs of the trading of pollution allowances.

At present, surveys show that utility companies are tending towards over-compliance with the new standards – mostly by installing new technology to remove sulphur dioxide from flue gas, and some through fuel switching. The inclination to over-comply means that there will be extra allowances for sale. The price of allowances or 'permits to pollute' should therefore be kept pretty low.

In Phase 1, which runs from 1995 to the year 2000, 110 of the dirtiest plants have been targeted to reduce their emissions. Because most of these power stations are likely to install new technology to reduce emissions in preference to buying extra pollution allowances, the price of pollution permits will probably continue to remain low throughout Phase 1. But after the year 2000, in Phase 2, a permanent annual cap of 8.9m tonnes of sulphur dioxide will be applied to all the electricity generators. Assuming that demand for electricity increases, many power stations will find they are unable to meet demand while keeping within the pollution ceiling – solely by installing clean technology. To meet demand for power, they will have to purchase extra pollution allowances. In Phase 2 allowance prices are expected to rise to about $600 per tonne. This compares with $250–$300 per tonne in the first deal. The EPA's penalty for emitting excess sulphur dioxide in $2 000 per tonne.

1. Explain briefly why economists regard the formation of acid rain as a 'market failure'? [4 marks]
2. Explain (a) the statement that the electricity market is a 'regulatory-driven market', and (b) how consumers might benefit from the trading of pollution allowances. [3, 3 marks]
3. With the aid of supply and demand analysis, explain why, according to the passage, the price of pollution permits or allowances is likely to rise from $250–$300 per allowance in Phase 1 to about $600 in Phase 2. [6 marks]
4. The passage states that: 'The national cap on sulphur dioxide emissions will be achieved in the most economically efficient way by trading the rights to pollute…'.

   (a) Briefly describe *one* other method, besides the creation of a market in pollution permits, by which sulphur dioxide pollution might be limited. [2 marks]

   (b) Discuss the advantages and disadvantages of the various methods of controlling sulphur dioxide pollution. [7 marks]

Chapter Six

Externalities 2: external benefits

' "*A cat may look at a king,*" *said Alice.*' Lewis Carroll

External benefits

Externalities were defined in the previous chapter where external costs were analysed. Here we turn to **external benefits**, their causes and consequences and how allocative efficiency can be attained where they exist. Much of the discussion turns on the provision of **public goods** and **mixed goods**. Where externalities cannot explain public provision we turn to distribution and equity arguments.

External benefits, like external costs, are by-products of production and consumption. They are positive side-effects which raise welfare. As with external costs there may be *producer-to-producer* effects, such as skills training which workers take with them when they move; *producer-to-consumer effects*; and *consumer-to-consumer effects*, such as a well-maintained house which enhances the value of the house next door. Many external benefits, from services like public transport, education or refuse collection, come from simultaneous consumption and production.

The extract in the box entitled 'The Harrogate Conference Centre: they meant well' illustrates external benefits. You might consider the questions posed in the last few lines of the extract.

Goods that provide external benefits are known as mixed goods and are under-provided by the market. Mixed goods are a sub-category of public goods, the main category being pure public goods. These are goods which in effect are all externality because none of their benefits can be confined to those prepared to pay. The best known example is national defence. The precise attributes which make goods public goods are discussed later in this chapter.

External benefits and misallocation

Where there were external costs we found that there was over-provision; conversely, where there are external benefits, there is under-provision. There is allocative inefficiency because the market fails to provide some units of the good or service for which social benefits exceed social costs. Figure 13 on page 58 shows how this happens.

In Figure 13, assuming that there are no external costs, private and

The Harrogate Conference Centre: they meant well

Since its days as a spa, Harrogate has lived off visitors. In the 1970s it seemed common sense to complement its existing exhibition halls with an up-to-date centre for the booming conference business.

The original, mid-1970s estimate was just under £8 million. The final cost, agreed only this month, after six years of operation, was £34 million – a worse-than-Concorde burden for its owner, a modest district council.

If only Harrogate were Labour-run Islington, free-marketeers in Brighton this week – at the Conservative party conference – would have had yet another wondrous case of town-hall lunacy to make fun of. But it is not: Harrogate has been Conservative-run throughout.

And for all the errors of execution, local Tories still argue that the intention was sound.

The conference centre was built, and is run even now, quite specifically to benefit the local community as a whole, not just to show bottom-line profit for its owners. The centre and its halls are well filled, by industry standards; consultants suggest that they bring £50–60 million a year into the area. Their future may well lie in private ownership or at least private management. But would the centre ever have got off the ground if the council had not built it? If not, ought it to have remained unbuilt? The answers are not as self-evident in Harrogate as in Brighton.

The Economist, 15 October 1988

social costs are the same. So the supply curve – marginal private costs – also represents marginal social costs. The market demand curve is the sum of all consumers' marginal benefit (utility) curves which are marginal private benefits (MPB) only. However, the production and consumption of the good or service, say public transport, gives benefits (emptier roads and less pollution) to other road users and people who live near traffic routes. These are external benefits and do not enter the private demand schedule. They are shown by the marginal external benefit schedule (MXB). Marginal external benefits are *estimated* because demand for external benefits is not known (see on to 'Public goods' for why this is so).

Social benefits include all benefits, private and external, and are shown in the diagram as the marginal social benefit schedule (MSB). For each unit MSB is obtained by adding together private and external benefits: for unit q' private benefits are $q'f$, external benefits are $q'd$, and social benefits are $q'g$, which is external benefits ($fg = q'd$) added to private benefits. Thus the marginal social benefit (MSB) curve is marginal external benefits (MXB) added vertically to marginal private benefits (MPB).

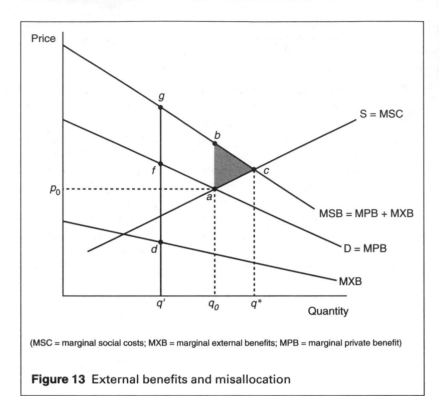

(MSC = marginal social costs; MXB = marginal external benefits; MPB = marginal private benefit)

Figure 13 External benefits and misallocation

The private market leads to production at q_0, where the supply and demand curves intersect at a; but at q_0 and beyond there are units which add more to social benefits than to social cost. For maximum welfare (**allocative efficiency**) every unit up to q^* should be produced. The **deadweight loss** which arises from the market's failure to take account of external benefits is shown by the excess of social benefit over social cost for each unit between q_0 and q^* and is the shaded area abc.

Public goods

Public goods are part of a spectrum which ranges from pure public goods to pure private goods, with mixed goods in-between. There is no market demand curve for a public good; this, and the consequent allocative inefficiency, comes about because of the special characteristics of public goods.

Consumption of a private good is *rival* – my eating an apple prevents you from eating it. Exclusion from benefit of those not prepared to pay is possible – if you will not pay for the apple the seller will keep it (i.e. will exclude you). However, a public good is not like an apple:

- *either* consumption is non-rival
- *or* exclusion is not feasible
- *or* both of these characteristics are present.

First, consider **non-rival consumption**. This means that an additional consumer adds nothing to cost. For example, an additional pedestrian on a well-lit street does not add to the cost of lamp-posts, lights and electricity; or an additional car crossing an uncrowded bridge adds nothing to cost. (It would be different if the bridge were crowded, when it would add to congestion which imposes time and fuel costs.) Being able to see the road at night, or being able to cross a river adds to consumer welfare without adding anything to cost.

For allocative efficiency, that is to maximize welfare, every consumer who wishes to use the bridge (up to the point where it becomes congested) should be able to do so. A toll, though feasible, would be inefficient since it would reduce welfare by preventing some people from using the bridge, without any matching cost reduction. If the toll charge were £1, everyone who valued crossing at less than that amount would not cross, and would be deprived of 95 pence-worth or 60 pence-worth, and so on, of benefit. For maximum welfare goods with a marginal cost of consumption of zero (MC = 0) should have a price equal to zero (*p* = MC). No private firm would undertake the production of a good for which price is zero. A private bridge owner would charge a toll which would be allocatively inefficient because it would deter potential beneficiaries without saving any costs. (It must be noted that it is the **marginal cost of consumption** which is zero; the **marginal cost of production** of these goods is not zero: the cost of an additional *consumer* of street lighting is zero, but the cost of an additional *street light* is positive.)

The second characteristic of a public good is *non-exclusion*. Non-exclusion means that it is not feasible to exclude non-payers from benefit. Here it is not the case, as with the bridge, that market provision is undesirable; it is rather that market provision is impossible. Take national defence or clean streets as examples. Most people want their country to be defended and to walk in litter-free streets. However, if these services are provided then even those not prepared to pay benefit. An individual will reason: 'Why should I pay if my neighbour who refuses to pay benefits equally? I won't pay.' If everyone wants to be a **free-rider** like this – and where numbers are large this is what happens – then preferences are not revealed and the service is not provided.

As well as national defence, street lights and empty bridges, public goods also include law and order (provided by the combined services of police, law courts and prisons), flood protection, roads, national parks, and medical and other research.

- For some of them consumption is non-rival and exclusion is not feasible – for example street lights, and national parks when uncongested.
- For others, though, exclusion is feasible and consumption is non-rival – for example an uncongested motorway.
- For others consumption is rival but exclusion is not feasible – for example busy city roads, though electronic road pricing will change this.

Externalities are non-rival and non-excludable. A public good is, in effect, all externality, and so there is no private demand schedule. This does not mean, however, as is sometimes argued, that there is 'joint' demand for public goods. People do not jointly or collectively demand street lights or law and order: as with any good, *individuals* have preferences for them – they are in individuals' preference functions. A nuclear disarmer's preferences for defence would be very different from those of a person who wanted 'strong defences'. Society's demand for defence is the sum of many different individual preferences; this is true for all public goods.

Finally, it should be made clear that public goods are goods for which the market fails, either completely or in part. Public sector ownership of plant and equipment, and organization of production, does not make the output a public good. For example, postal services are produced within the public sector, but they are private goods. Before privatization the same was true of coal, electricity, gas and telecommunications.

Mixed goods

Mixed goods, as the name suggests, provide a mixture of private and external benefits. *Like private goods they are rival in consumption and are excludable.* For example, if I am in a hospital bed receiving treatment you cannot use that bed, so you as an extra patient add to cost; and if you cannot provide evidence of your ability to pay you could be refused treatment (excluded). Therefore preferences are revealed and the market works.

However, *mixed goods also give non-rival, non-excludable external benefits for which preferences are not revealed.* Only private benefits are reflected in market demand and, as the first section of this chapter showed, the market under-provides.

Health care, education, public transport, refuse collection and the fire service are all mixed goods. The balance of private benefit and external benefit varies between them. For health care it seems likely that the balance is fairly heavily weighted towards private benefits, with the person who receives treatment gaining more than the community; but there are protective side-effects (against infectious disease) and productive side-effects (getting workers back to work). Some claim that education, too, provides only small external benefits, but others take an opposing view, arguing that a well-educated workforce raises productivity, exports and economic growth, which benefits everyone in an economy.

For public transport the balance between private, internal benefits and external benefits moves towards a fairly large proportion of external benefits, particularly in large cities where a good public system keeps the whole city moving. Every individual and business in the city benefits, whether they use public transport or not. Similarly a good national rail network benefits business, road users and the whole economy. The Director General of the British Institute of Management recently remarked:

> 'Continued emphasis on the primacy of private transport will eventually work against the interest of the majority of users – and of the efficiency of the UK as a whole.'

Finally, the fire service is an example of a mixed good where external benefits are likely to outweigh internal. If firefighters put out a blaze in a chemical factory they benefit not only the chemical firm but also a large surrounding area which they save from explosions and pollution. If they put out a fire in a single flat they may save from fire every apartment in the same building.

The role for government

● Pure public goods

Where the market fails completely the public sector must provide. For efficiency it should provide in line with people's preferences, which is where demand (MSB) and supply (we assume, MSC) curves intersect.

However, though there could be market supply schedules for street lights, defence goods, flood protection and so on, there is no possibility of market demand schedules for them. *This is not because individual demand does not exist but because it is not revealed.* If people could be persuaded to reveal their preferences, to show what they would pay for different quantities of each public good, then a market demand schedule could be constructed. Market demand could interact with market supply and an efficient level of output could be arrived at.

However, such demand schedules do not exist. In democracies governments determine public provision. At election times people vote for the party whose public spending and taxation plans are most in line with their preferences.

Whether or not the outcome is that public goods are provided in line with majority preferences is a matter of debate. Some economists have argued that biases in the democratic process lead to under-provision, a smaller quantity of public goods than people really want.

- Pigou, for example, thought that people take account only of internal benefits when voting.
- Galbraith ('private affluence and public squalor') thought that people would favour private goods, which are associated with the merits of the market, over public goods, damned by association with the state.
- Others, public choice economists and the political Right, argue that there are biases which lead to over-provision and more public expenditure than people really want. They think that this happens because the benefits are obvious to voters but that the costs are not: voters think that others will pay the taxes which buy public goods.

Once the overall size of the public budget and each spending programme has been decided, then **cost–benefit analysis** (CBA) may be used to determine whether a particular project should be undertaken or to choose between alternative projects. *CBA is an efficiency technique which assesses both costs and benefits; it takes into account external as well as internal effects and looks ahead into the future:* CBA takes 'a wide view and a long view'. However, CBA may be used to support a project that has already been selected on political grounds, such as a particular route for a new road.

- ### Mixed goods
Here the government's function is again to try to provide the optimum quantity in line with external as well as private demand. This is shown in Figure 14.

The market quantity is q_0 at price p_0. The efficient, welfare maximizing quantity is q^*, which would happen if price to the buyer were lower at p_b, and price to the seller were higher, at p_s. To achieve this a subsidy is necessary, of size s, the difference between supply price and demand price at q^*. The new demand curve, including the subsidy, is the broken line D_sD_s. Again the qualification must be made: it is easy to draw a schedule showing external effects and to show the optimum quantity of output. In practice external benefits are very difficult to quantify and to put a value on.

Figure 14 could represent the demand and supply curves for bus services in a city, together with an estimate of the external benefits of those services and of the size of subsidy required. For other mixed goods – in particular education, but also health care in many countries – rather than subsidy there is free public provision paid for by taxation. In this case, for efficiency, the government should aim to provide the welfare maximizing quantity in line with private and external preferences.

We should note that in drawing a marginal external benefit (MXB) curve, both here and in Figure 13, we have assumed away the difficulties noted earlier about the revelation of preferences for benefits which are non-excludable. The MXB curve is the external beneficiaries pseudo-demand curve for, say, public transport. This pseudo-demand curve cannot be known, but in the case of public transport some quantification of external benefits, value of time saved, fuel saved and so on, is possible.

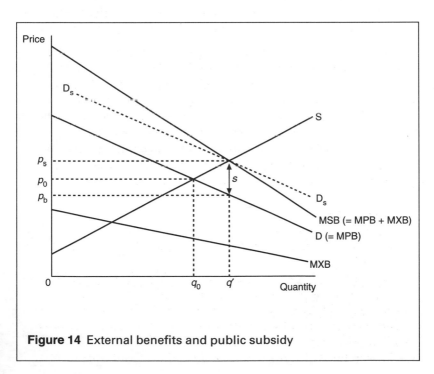

Figure 14 External benefits and public subsidy

Equity and merit goods

New Right economists dispute much of the argument on mixed goods and claim that the external benefits from education and health care, in particular, are very small, and no justification for public provision. Some economists who are not on the political Right tend to agree that these services' external benefits are not large, so that they cannot be used to justify state provision. However, this does not lead them to conclude, as do the New Right, that health care and education should be left to the market. They argue that individual preferences about the kind of society we want to live in provide the justification for public provision. If the majority want children to be educated and access to health care to depend on need rather than on the ability to pay for it, then a democratic society will provide this. *This argument is based on equity not on efficiency.*

Finally something needs to be said about what are termed 'merit goods'. These are goods that are so 'meritorious' that the government overrides consumer preferences and provides the quantity which it thinks people ought to consume. Health care and education, which are mixed goods, may also be classified as merit goods. There are no efficiency arguments here, no economic analysis about efficiency underlies the concept of merit goods. We should think of them as redistribution in kind. It is argued that taxpayers are more prepared to provide free education and health care than cash benefits.

Though some goods fall into both the mixed and the merit goods categories there is a clear distinction between the two and the terms should not be used interchangeably. In the case of mixed goods the function of the public sector is to provide the efficient quantity, in line with consumers' preferences, both internal and external. In the case of merit goods there are no efficiency arguments, and consumers' preferences may be overruled.

KEY WORDS

External benefits	Marginal cost of consumption
Public goods	Marginal cost of production
Mixed goods	Free-rider
Allocative efficiency	Cost–benefit analysis
Deadweight loss	Merit goods
Non-rival consumption	

Reading list
Hurl, B., Chapters 2 and 3 in *Privatization and the Public Sector*, 3rd edn, Heinemann Educational, 1995.

Smith, D., Chapter 3 in *UK Current Economic Policy*, Heinemann Educational, 1994.

Essay topics
1. The UK's technical expertise makes possible a relatively cheap means of disposing of toxic waste, so: 'The USA is to pay British Nuclear Fuels half a million dollars to import and reprocess over 183 000 gallons of nitric acid contaminated with uranium from the US atomic weapons plant.' – *The Independent*, 12 August 1994
   (a) Distinguish between public goods, merit goods and private goods and consider into which classification the reprocessing of atomic waste should be put. [15 marks]
   (b) Will this activity produce gains from trade? [10 marks]
   [University of Cambridge Local Examinations Syndicate, 1996]
2. Explain, with the aid of examples, the main characteristics of (i) public goods; (ii) merit goods. [5, 5 marks]
   (b) To what extent is it desirable that the government should provide (i) public goods; (ii) merit goods? [6, 9 marks]
   [Associated Examining Board 1994]
3. (a) Outline the main characteristics of a free market economy. [20 marks]
   (b) What are the main advantages of market forces as a means of allocating resources? [30 marks]
   (c) Examine the problems that might arise if health care and education were provided solely by market forces. [50 marks]
   [University of London Examinations and Assessment Council 1996]

Data Response Question
This task is based on a question set by the Oxford and Cambridge Schools Examination Board in 1993. Study Tables A and B on page 66 which are Department of Education figures for sources of finance available to students in higher education. Then answer the questions.

Table A Annual student maintenance grants and loans (£)

	Maximum maintenance grant (means-tested)			Maximum student loan (not means-tested)		
	1990–91 (actual)	1991–92 (actual)	2007–8 (planned)	1990–91 (actual)	1991–92 (actual)	2007–8 (planned)
Away from home and studying in London	2845	2845	2845	460	660	2845
Away from home and studying elsewhere	2265	2265	2265	420	580	2265
Living at parental home	1795	1795	1795	330	460	1795

Table B Parental contributions (£) to student finance, 1991–92

Parents' residual income*	Parental contribution†
Below 12 650	Nil
12 650	45 (minimum)
15 000	274
20 000	912
25 000	1638
30 000	2493
35 000	3348
40 000	4203
45 000	5057
49 343	5800 (maximum)

*Residual income is gross income minus pension and some life insurance payments, interest payments allowed for tax purposes, and allowance for adult dependent relatives.
†Total contribution can exceed the maximum maintenance grant where there are two or more children in higher education.

Department of Education

1. What do the data reveal about the economic principles governing the financing of students in higher education? [10 marks]
2. What are the likely consequences of the gradual change in the balance between maintenance grants and student loans? [15 marks]

Chapter Seven

Supply side economics

' "The rule is, jam tomorrow and jam yesterday – but never jam today." '   Lewis Carroll

Supply side economics and supply side policies were developed in the 1970s. They were part of the revival of classical economics that focused on the efficiency of the free market and on the desirability of minimizing government intervention. Supply side policies were introduced into the UK from 1979 onwards by Margaret Thatcher's Conservative administrations.

If equity had been given some attention in the post-1945 Keynesian/Beveridge world (see Chapter 8 on the welfare state), then in the 1980s efficiency was given priority. Supply side policies promoting efficiency lead to conflict with equity.

The supply side
The supply side is the real side of the economy where production takes place. Behind the aggregate supply curve is the economy's **production function** and the **labour market**. It is firms and their workers engaged in the output of goods and services.

Output depends on resources – human (labour) and non-human (mainly capital). Increasing the quantity and quality of output involves increasing the quantity and quality of inputs and the way they are combined in production. To boost the supply side and increase output requires, in the short run:

- a larger proportion of the population in work
- longer hours of work
- more effort;

and in the longer run:

- better education and training
- more efficient plant and equipment
- new products and processes.

The production function, which shows how output rises when the labour input is increased, depicts the short run when capital and technology are unchanged. In the longer run, when these change, the function will shift. The companion book in this series, *Supply side economics*, explains the economic model in more detail.

Sources of higher output

Changes that lead to higher output may be put into two categories:

- short run, exhaustible, measures;
- longer run, sustainable, measures.

The short run measures are principally tax and social security changes that shift the labour supply schedule outward and raise employment and hence output.

Long run measures, which affect both labour and capital, shift up the production function.

● Higher output in the short run (exhaustible measures)

In the short run it is possible to increase output, even when the production function remains fixed, by increasing the quantity of variable input – labour. Supply-siders argue that there are policies that achieve this: measures to make 'workers more willing to work'. Principally these are policies that make work monetarily more rewarding – they make for a larger gap between out-of-work income and in-work income.

- Cuts in benefits for the unemployed reduce income when out of work, and cuts in income tax make take-home pay higher. These measures reduce the **replacement rate**, the ratio of out-of-work income to in-work income.
- Changing the law to make trade unions less powerful also makes workers less likely to take action against employers, less likely to strike, and more likely to maintain work effort.

These are one-off, exhaustible, measures. There are limits to cuts in income tax, and there are levels of income below which unemployed people and their families in a developed economy cannot be expected to live. Once tax rates and unemployment benefit levels and rules have been altered to make workers think that work is always preferable to unemployment, then this policy has been exhausted. Output can be raised no more by increasing the labour input. However, longer run, sustainable measures are still available.

● Higher output in the longer run (sustainable measures)

Sustainable supply side policies require measures that operate in the longer run. These are policies that shift the production function:

- increases in investment which increase the quantity of capital equipment;

- research and development which leads to technical change and improvements in the quality of capital;
- policies that improve the quality of labour – improvement in education and training at all levels from nursery education and basic literacy and numeracy skills to post-school skills training and to higher and postgraduate education. The government's skills audit (see box 'The unskilled nation') shows how much the UK needs to improve.

The unskilled nation

SIR HUMPHREY APPLEBY, the slippery civil servant in the BBC's political comedy series "Yes Minister", would have called it "courageous" – ie, foolhardy. After 17 years in office, and a matter of months before an election, the government has published a detailed study admitting that education and skill levels in Britain are below those in Germany, France, America and Singapore. Unsurprisingly, Labour said it was a damning indictment of the government's record. Gillian Shephard, the education and employment secretary, hopes that voters will recall that, until recently, Labour opposed many of the government's school reforms. She has also announced a package of further reforms in response to the study's findings.

The study, published on June 13th as part of the annual white paper on competitiveness, compared the qualifications held by the British population with those in the four other countries, chosen as key "economic competitors". This "skills audit" found that only 45% of British adults have qualifications that are at least equivalent of GCSE grade "C" in maths, English and one other subject, worse than all the other countries. The figure for Germany is 70%. Multinational firms were asked to compare their workers in each country. Confirming the findings of other recent studies, they reported that the British came bottom of the class at sums.

Abridged from *The Economist* 15 June 1995

Improvements in the quantity and quality of capital equipment, and in the education and training of workers, raises labour productivity. The total product of labour rises – the aggregate production function moves to a higher level. As labour becomes more productive employers demand more of it.

As these longer term measures take effect, aggregate output rises. Supply side measures, when they involve improvement in labour and in capital equipment, making labour more productive, can raise output, employment and the real wage.

Supply side policies in the UK

The term 'supply side policies' was not used until the later 1970s. Measures with this label were introduced after the Conservative's general election victory in 1979. They were aimed at encouraging efficiency and economic growth by promoting free markets and reducing government intervention in the economy.

Keynesian governments before 1979 had intervened on the supply side to promote economic growth. Their rationale, however, was market failure and the necessity for government intervention to correct this (see Chapter 3 in Healey and Cook, *Supply side economics*).

The 'supply-siders' of the political Right now took precisely the opposite standpoint. Based on New Classical economics, their policies to boost output and employment took as their starting point the efficiency of free markets and the stultifying effect of government intervention. In the 1980s supply side policies were aimed at reducing the role of government by renouncing 'destabilizing' demand management, by reducing taxes, by privatizing and deregulating. The intention was to give incentives to workers and to free the entrepreneurial energies of the private sector.

- ● Labour market policies
There were reductions in income tax, social security and minimum wages. There was new union legislation, and wages councils were abolished.

Between 1979 and 1988 the top marginal rate of income tax on earned income was reduced from 83 to 40 per cent, and the basic rate from 33 to 25 per cent. However, other taxes were raised to maintain total government revenues. In particular in 1979 the standard rate of VAT was increased from 8 to 15 per cent.

Unemployment benefits were reduced by abolishing earnings-related supplements, by taxing benefits, and by linking benefit increases to price inflation – not to wage inflation which is higher. Consequently the short-term replacement rate – the ratio of out-of-work income to in-work income – fell from 75 to 60 per cent on average. The intention was to make workers prepared to take work at lower wages – to shift the labour supply curve outwards (downwards).

At the same time as the government was implementing tax and social security measures aimed at making workers more responsive to market forces, they were also abolishing wages councils, which set minimum wages in low-paid industries. Trade union power was reduced by a variety of Employment Acts in 1980, 82, 84, 88, and 90 – see Chapter 5 in *Supply side economics*. These measures were all intended to reduce non-market forces in the labour market and to make the labour supply more flexible, 'more willing to work'.

● **Longer term supply side measures**
New Classical economics stresses the importance of competitive markets and the profit motive to spur entrepreneurs to seek efficient production methods and to introduce new products and new processes. In pursuit of enlarging the role of the private sector and market forces the principal policies were:

● denationalization;
● deregulation;
● franchising.

Sometimes the term **privatization** is used as a general term to cover all these measures (as in the box), while sometimes it is used solely to mean denationalization.

PRIVATIZATION

Denationalization is the sale of state-owned companies to the private sector – to individual shareholders, to insurance companies, unit trusts and pensions funds where small savers put their money. Companies sold include: British Telecom, British Gas, British Airways, British Steel, regional water companies, electricity generation and supply, British Coal, Railtrack and many others.

Deregulation is the removal of legal barriers to entry to a previously protected market to encourage competition. Examples are bus services, telecommunication, gas and electricity production.

Franchising/competitive tendering is the situation where the public sector continues to pay for the provision of a service but the private sector undertakes the organization of production. There is competitive tendering by private firms who compete for contracts from local authorities, central government departments and the NHS. This is intended to drive down costs. Contracted-out services include: refuse collection, cleaning and catering services, vehicle maintenance and grounds maintenance.

Along with privatization, intended to encourage entrepreneurship, and response to the profit motive, Conservative tax reform also included:

- the reduction of corporation tax, from 52 to 35 per cent;
- labour market reforms to increase occupational and geographical labour mobility (see Chapter 5 in *Supply side economics*, 3rd edn).

Supply side policies: outcomes and conflicts

- Tax and social security reforms

If we allow that there might have been some efficiency gains – incentive effects – from the tax reforms of the 1980s, the cost of these gains was greater inequality of post-tax incomes, and so less equity. *Whereas income tax can take account of a taxpayer's ability to pay, with higher rates for those with higher incomes, expenditure taxes, levied at the point of sale, are at the same rate on everyone regardless of income.*

Over the period 1978 to 1990, income tax revenues fell from 35 per cent of total tax receipts to 27 per cent, and VAT receipts increased from 10 to 17 per cent of the total. Hence the tax system became more **regressive**. It took proportionately more from those with lower incomes and proportionately less from those with higher incomes than before the reforms. If tax in proportion to income or tax progression is regarded as equitable, then equity was reduced in the 1980s.

FOR RICHER, FOR POORER

Key results of the study of UK living standards include:

- The increase in income inequality during the 1980s dwarfed the fluctuations in inequality seen in previous decades.
- Whilst real incomes (before housing costs) have grown by around 84 per cent on average over the last three decades, the incomes of the richest tenth have risen twice as fast (up 113 per cent) as those of the poorest tenth (58 per cent).
- The real incomes of the poorest tenth ranked by income after housing costs were at a peak in 1979 at £73 per week, but by 1991 the real incomes of the poorest tenth were much lower than this, at just over £61 per week (both in January 1994 prices). This represented a return to the living standards of a quarter of a century earlier.

From A.Goodman and S.Webb, 'For richer for poorer: the changing distribution of income in the UK, 1961–91', *Fiscal Studies*, November 1994

Lower social security benefits also made for greater income inequalities. Whether these had any marked incentive effects is open to question. Keynesians have suggested that what reduces employment is insufficient demand and hence the lack of jobs, rather than the lack of willingness to work on the part of the unemployed. The box entitled 'For richer, for poorer' shows some of the key results of a study undertaken by researchers at the Institute of Fiscal Studies into changes in UK income distribution, and a large part of what happened to incomes at the bottom of the distribution in the 1980s was the result of supply side reforms.

● Union reform and wages councils abolition
The abolition of wages councils and the 1980s trade union legislation altered the balance of power in the labour market – workers lost power and employers gained it. Union membership and days lost in strikes both fell. In some industries wages costs were reduced, in others employers were able to introduce new technology and new ways of working, and shed jobs.

Productivity and efficiency *were* increased, but the cost was borne by those whose real wages did not keep pace with the average, those who lost their jobs, and those whose job security was reduced.

'The UK labour market has become more like the US labour market – more flexible, but at the cost of lower wages for the worst-off, and lower incomes when out of work. ... America's labour market delivers more employment, and therefore more output ... than Europe's; ... but the price is worse poverty in and out of work, and greater economic insecurity.

The Economist, 12 March 1994

● Privatization
The consequencies of denationalization, deregulation and contracting-out include efficiency gains – some clear, some doubtful – and greater inequality in society – gains for the better-off and losses for the worse-off.

It cannot be claimed that denationalization was the sole cause of greater efficiency in the corporations that were privatized. Other things were happening in the 1980s that also led to these effects, including rationalization, downsizing, and the pursuit of efficiency driven by international competition. It is often pointed out that British Steel achieved its efficiency/productivity gains in the early 1980s while still within the public sector. Surpluses accruing from the power of **natural monopolies** – which are often one step ahead of the regulators in protecting their monopoly power – now go to private shareholders and as rewards for executives, rather than to taxpayers in general.

The extract 'A winning team' illustrates some of the issues: greater efficiency at the cost of fewer jobs and lower rewards. In this example efficiency is achieved within the public sector, though under the threat of private sector competition. The lower costs that competitive tendering produces are, in part, borne by workers, part-time cleaners for example, whose wages and conditions of work are worsened. It was not only post-tax income inequality which rose in the 1980s, the pre-tax income distribution also became more unequal, with low incomes falling further below the average and high incomes rising further above it. Moreover there is no unanimity that contracting-out always increased efficiency. For example Flemming and Oppenheimer of the Cambridge-based Clare group of economists claim that contracting out has had 'questionable efficiency gains' and may have reduced quality in some services (*National Institute Economic Review*, July 1996).

A WINNING TEAM

Turning Lewisham's in-house direct service organisation into a group which was able to win against private sector competition was not achieved without pain. Many jobs were shed in the drive to make the council's services fit for compulsory competitive tendering.

On one occasion three managers took out a refuse lorry and spent a day collecting rubbish to prove that three people could do work that had required eight.

The drive for efficiency is continuing. In order to remain competitive, all staff and managers have just lost one week's annual holiday, and sick pay – apart from the statutory element – has been withdrawn for the first week of every absence.

Adapted from *Financial Times,* 24 May 1995

Both the short-term social security and tax changes and the longer term privatization measures were aimed at promoting greater efficiency. To a greater or lesser extent – consider the poor performance of Yorkshire Water, for example – this was achieved, but at the cost of greater inequality in society. The defence of the supply-siders to the charge that their reforms would make the rich richer and the poor poorer was that there would be a **'trickle down' effect** in a dynamic economy which would benefit the poor – jam today and tomorrow for everyone. From the evidence, like that in 'For richer, for poorer', this does not appear to have happened.

KEY WORDS

Production function	Competitive tendering
Labour market	Regressive
Replacement rate	Natural monopolies
Privatization	Trickle down effect

Reading list

Healey, N., and Cook, M., *Supply side economics*, 3rd edn, Heinemann Educational, 1996.

Hurl, B., *Privatization and the Public Sector*, 3rd edn, Heinemann Educational, 1995.

Simpson, L., and Paterson, I., *The UK Labour Market*, Heinemann Educational, 1994.

Essay topics

1. Explain the basis for supply side measures to cure unemployment. Discuss whether or not the principal measures taken by the government to deal with unemployment in recent years have been successful [25 marks]

   [Northern Examinations and Assessment Board 1995]

2. Examine the implications for the UK labour market of any *three* of the following: (i) the introduction of maximum working hours; (ii) the introduction of a national minimum wage; (iii) a reduction in state benefits to unemployed persons; (iv) the introduction of child care allowances for working parents. [100 marks]

   [University of London Examinations and Assessment Council 1995]

3. Do you agree that any programme of privatization which merely replaces a public monopoly with a private monopoly is a failure? [25 marks]

   [University of Cambridge Local Examinations Syndicate 1996]

4. (a) How is the performance of an economy affected by both the geographical and the occupational mobility of labour? [12 marks]

   (b) Outline the various ways in which the government can seek to improve the mobility of labour and critically evaluate the

arguments for and against such intervention by the government.
[13 marks]
[Associated Examining Board 1996]

Data Response Question

This task is based on a question set by the University of London
Examinations and Assessment Council in 1996. Read the following
article which is adapted from 'The role of the regulators', published in
The Economist on 1 June 1991. Then answer the questions.

The regulation of privatized industries

Big profits mean bad regulation. Or so you would think from the outcry
that greeted British Telecom's announcement that its profits in 1990–91
were £31.1 billion, which is equivalent to £97 per second. Much of the
current uproar is due to a simple confusion between big – which the
monopoly's profits certainly are – and too big. BT is Britain's biggest,
most valuable and most profitable firm. But its profits are a relatively small
proportion of sales (at 21.5 per cent) and of capital (21.3 per cent).

Even so, some of the privatized monopolies' profits may well be too
high. The regulators certainly think so. Their main method of control is the
pricing formula known as 'RPI minus X'. This means that each firm must
limit its price rises to 'X' percentage points less than the rate of inflation. If
the regulator reckons that a firm is earning too much monopoly profit, it
can raise 'X'. So far, the regulators have raised 'X' each time they have
reviewed it.

This is no surprise. To get public sector managers to agree to be privatized, and to persuade investors to buy the shares, the government had
to offer incentives to the newly-privatized companies. In the case of the
water companies, managers were encouraged to believe that they would
be able to raise their prices to cover the costs of almost any investment.
Once privatized, the government has little reason to preserve such a
friendly policy and every reason to make life tougher since consumers
are voters.

'RPI minus X' can work if the regulator has a good idea of how efficient
the firm is, and how much better it could be. This is most likely when technology is fairly mature, so that the rate at which the regulators learn about
the firm is faster than the rate at which the firm changes. In most of
Britain's regulated monopolies, technology changes slowly as with gas
pipes, water pipes, runways and so on. The big exception is telecommunications, where technology is changing fast.

Promoting competition should be the aim of the regulators, even in technologically mature industries. Britain still lacks a clear policy on vertical integration. Electricity has been broken into competitive generation and monopoly distributors, but gas and telecommunications remain more integrated. 'Yardstick' competition – comparing the performance of one local monopoly with other similar monopolies – has been considered by the regulators for some time, but it has still to be seriously used. 'Unbundling' the costs and prices of all a firm's activities – as BT began to do when it charged for directory enquiries and cut ordinary call charges – reduced unnecessary regulation and should go much further.

1. Discuss the factors that a regulator might take into account when deciding whether or not the profits made by a utility such as BT or a water company are too high. [7 marks]
2. Using the example of *either* gas *or* telecommunications, explain and illustrate the term 'vertical integration'. [4 marks]
3. Discuss the advantages and disadvantages of breaking up the electricity industry into separate companies for generating and distributing electricity. [6 marks]
4. Examine the possible effects on the efficiency of a privatized utility of *one* of the following regulatory policy measures referred to in the passage: (a) the 'RPI minus X' pricing rule; (b) 'yardstick' competition; (c) 'unbundling' costs and prices. [8 marks]

Chapter Eight
Welfare state economics

' *"Fair play with the cake, you know," said the Lion.*'   Lewis Carroll

The term 'welfare state' refers to the state's responsibility for the welfare of its citizens through the delivery of cash incomes and services in kind. In the UK the four principal welfare services are:

- **social security** – cash benefits to prevent or relieve poverty;
- **education** – primary, secondary, further and higher education;
- **health care** – principally via the National Health Service;
- **public sector housing.**

Spending on these four services amounts to over half of government spending and is between 20 and 25 per cent of the total output of the economy.

BEVERIDGE

The modern British welfare state dates back to the Beveridge Report, *Report on Social Insurance and Allied Services,* published in 1942 during the Second World War. In the relative social cohesion of the war years people determined that 'never again' should there be a return to the misery of the 1930s, and the Beveridge Report gave shape to these ideas.

Beveridge identified 'five giant evils of Want, Disease, Squalor, Ignorance and Idleness', and to fight each evil, 'five giants on the road to reconstruction': social security, a national health service, housing, state education and a commitment to full employment.

Equity, efficiency and welfare

State provision of services in kind, such as health care, education and housing, and of **cash transfers** in the form of social security benefits, raise issues of equity and efficiency and of conflicts between the two principles.

• Services in kind

In Chapter 6 it was shown that goods and services that provide external benefits – mixed goods – are under-provided by the market. It may be argued that to a greater or a lesser degree health, education and public sector housing give benefits to those who are not direct consumers, so that it is efficient for the state to intervene and provide the welfare-maximizing quantity. Look again at Figure 13 in Chapter 6.

There are differences of opinion on the size of the external benefits from these services. It is likely that education provides fairly large benefits for the whole of society, including those who are no longer receiving any education. Hence the importance of the debate on the British education system and how it compares internationally: politicians and taxpayers are concerned not only with the quality of the experience of current pupils and students, but also with its effects on the whole of society and the economy and its productivity.

On the other hand, today much of the benefit of health care is *internal*. For example, recipients of treatment for asthma or heart disease personally receive most of the benefits, the rest of society much less – though, if a patient is able to work as a result of the treatment, society does save the invalidity benefit it might otherwise have to pay. Things were different when infectious diseases were rife: curing or vaccinating people who were ill or at risk of disease also gave protection to the rest of the population, so external benefits were potentially very large.

Moreover, health care for those of pensionable age, proportionately the largest consumers of the national health service, does not get the recipients of the care back to work and so cannot be justified on the grounds of externalities.

Public sector housing, when of good quality, may have beneficial social effects as well as the benefits it provides for its direct consumers. But, as with health care, these benefits are unlikely to be large. From the 1970s, and especially in the 1980s, there have been big changes in the way the government has helped with the provision of housing for those at the bottom of the income distribution. There has been a move away from direct subsidies to local authorities to help with the building of flats and houses – with tenants, whatever their incomes, paying lower than market rents. The shift has been away from 'bricks and mortar' towards subsidizing persons, by means of cash housing benefit to those on low incomes. At the same time there have been large cuts in public capital expenditure on housing.

If external benefits and efficiency do not justify state provision, then equity may do so – the provision of health, education and housing services represent income redistribution according to need. This redistribution in kind, the provision by the state of **merit goods,** is justified in a variety of ways, including the belief that taxpayers prefer to make 'gifts that are earmarked' rather than pay cash benefits which recipients may spend as they please.

Mixed goods and merit goods have been discussed in Chapter 6 and so they are taken no further in this chapter. However it is appropriate to consider briefly the changes that Conservative governments have made to their delivery in the 1980s and 90s – the introduction of internal markets in education and health care. The box 'Internal markets', adapted from David Smith's book in this series, *UK Current Economic Policy,* explains these reforms.

INTERNAL MARKETS

Perhaps the most far-reaching change of all in the welfare state has been the move to introduce internal markets.

In the NHS, general practitioners have been encouraged to become 'GP fundholders'. They have a choice between hospitals which compete on the basis of price, quality and waiting time. The market directs patients towards the most competitive GPs and hospitals. Hospitals need to hold down their prices to survive.

The state education system has also developed an internal market. Under the Local Management in Schools (LMS) initiative, schools have been encouraged to opt out of local authority control. Success depends on ability to attract pupils, who are directed to schools offering the best quality as defined by test results. As in any other market, those that do not offer a good service will go out of existence.

In terms of equity and efficiency there is disagreement over whether there have been gains:

- Against the efficiency gains of the health reforms must be set the higher administrative costs of the new system which have diverted resources from direct patient care. Whether efficiency gains have more than offset the higher costs is the area of dispute.
- There is inequity of treatment of patients depending on whether their GP is a fundholder or not, with patients of fundholders getting favourable treatment. This will disappear when, if it happens, all GPs become fundholders.
- In education it is claimed that parental choice is a misnomer. Parents may certainly express a *preference* for a certain school, but if a particular school is over-subscribed, rather than grow it may merely turn applicants away.

● Cash transfers

Transfer payments – cash social security benefits such as unemployment benefit and income support – involve decisions on trade-offs between equity and efficiency.

It is fair to provide incomes for people who have no jobs and for their dependants. However if raising taxes to pay benefits is a disincentive to taxpayers, and if benefit income deters people from seeking work, then what is fair may also be inefficient, because it reduces employment and output in the economy. The rest of the chapter is taken up with these issues.

Causes of poverty

People's incomes are determined by the resources they own and by the prices the market puts on the services of those resources. Though some own land and capital assets, for most people their main wealth is their own labour power (human capital) and their income is labour income (wages).

Poverty is caused by a lack of real resources, principally human capital. There may be no jobs, and a lack of skills and training usually makes available only low-paid employment at best. Old age, extreme youth, sickness or disability, or having young children to care for, make employment difficult or impossible. The causes of poverty are therefore linked to circumstances that put people with no other resources at a disadvantage in the labour market.

Until the 1980s the level of income support was an objective measure of the border between adequate subsistence and poverty. However, particularly since the separation of benefits from earnings, and the replacement of single payments by loans from the cash-limited Social Fund, many people consider that the state social security system no longer keeps everyone on benefits out of subsistence poverty.

Social security

Most people would agree that equity demands that there should be some redistribution of income to relieve poverty, though there are differences of view on which of the poor should be helped and how much help they should get. However, policies to reduce poverty may give rise to distortions that reduce total welfare. A fairer distribution of the cake might lead to a reduction in its size, and therefore be inefficient.

There are two principal ways of relieving poverty: fiscal methods and market intervention. We are not concerned here with market intervention, which involves policy measures like minimum wages, rent controls, and minimum prices for agricultural products.

Fiscal methods of poverty relief take us to the heart of the welfare state and its problems. On the one side are benefits, and on the other side are contributions and taxes to pay for them – social security.

Taxes and compulsory contributions to National Insurance funds, which are taxes under another name, are distortionary – they affect work incentives. Additionally on the transfers side, benefit payments also cause inefficiencies – for example the disincentive effects of the poverty trap.

Conflicts between equity and efficiency

The system operating today is different from the insurance system that Beveridge intended. Insured benefits are low or run out after a period of time, so that the unemployed, sick or old with no other income require additional benefits. This is means-tested, or 'targeted', or 'income related' help, called **income support**. *It is not a fall-back for the few but the main method of support for the many.* In addition, the insurance scheme is of no help to the low-paid in work, and there has been growth in the number and size of means-tested benefits paid to working households.

Many issues of equity and efficiency affect the benefits system. Consider first *the effectiveness of the system* in terms of achieving its objectives at minimum cost. This breaks down into:

- administrative efficiency, and
- efficiency in achieving the objectives, which will then also deliver equity.

Secondly consider *its effects on incentives*, and in particular:

- the unemployment trap, and
- the poverty trap.

● The effectiveness of the system

Does the system give the right benefits to the right people? Does it do so at minimum cost, with administrative efficiency?

Administrative efficiency

There is fairly wide agreement that the system is not administratively very efficient. This arises because there are a multiplicity of benefits and they are administered by more than one body. Most are managed by the Benefits Agency of the Department of Social Security (DSS), but housing benefit is dealt with by local authorities. For many claimants this means that the same information has to be collected twice.

Efficiency in achieving the objectives
Efficiency in achieving the aim of helping those in need is even more important than administrative efficiency. Inefficiency arises both from means-testing and from the complexity of benefits because both of these conditions lead to less than complete take-up. If those entitled to benefits do not get them, inefficiency leads to inequity.

● Effects of the system on incentives

The unemployment trap
Potential workers are in the **unemployment trap** when their out-of-work incomes are equal to, or higher than, their in-work incomes.

This situation can happen to a family whose wage-earner can command only low pay. Out-of-work benefits, income support, including support for spouse and children, and housing benefit, can be greater than potential earnings. In this situation rational 'economic man' would choose unemployment to employment, and would be in the unemployment trap.

The measure used to compare income in and out of work is the **replacement rate**. If the replacement rate is 0.85 then the person's income when out of work is 85 per cent of income when in work. Until recently the average short-term replacement rate, when unemployment benefit applied, was 60 per cent; the long-term rate is about 50 per cent.

Therefore *on average* the unemployment trap does not exist, because the unemployed on average nearly double their incomes on finding jobs. However there is always a distribution about the average, so for some the replacement rate will be below the average and for some it will be above. There will be a few, such as parents of families with only low earning potential, for whom the replacement rate will be 100 per cent or more.

It was to deal with this problem that **family credit**, a benefit designed to raise the incomes of low-paid families in work, was introduced. However family credit, which attempts to deal with the problem of the unemployment trap, worsens the problem of the **poverty trap**.

The poverty trap
This affects people who are in work. It deters them from attempting to work longer hours or harder, take more responsibility, seek promotion, to raise their income. This is because for every extra pound they earn they lose benefits, family credit and housing benefit, and have to

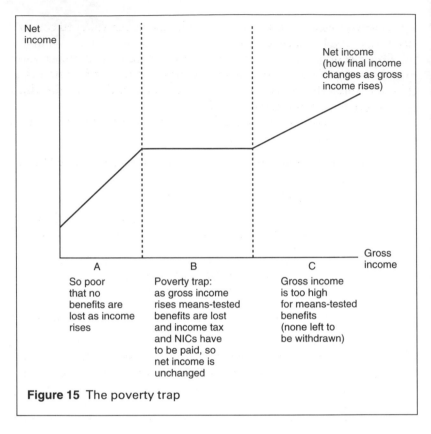

Net income

Net income
(how final income
changes as gross
income rises)

Gross
income

A

So poor
that no
benefits are
lost as income
rises

B

Poverty trap:
as gross income
rises means-tested
benefits are lost
and income tax
and NICs have
to be paid, so
net income is
unchanged

C

Gross income
is too high
for means-tested
benefits
(none left to
be withdrawn)

Figure 15 The poverty trap

pay income tax and National Insurance contributions. Out of the extra pound they earn they may get to keep just 4 pence. This represents an implicit tax rate on additional income of 96 per cent, far higher that the top marginal tax rate on high earners of 40 per cent. Figure 15 shows the poverty trap in diagrammatic form.

The poverty trap presents the efficiency versus equity dilemma in acute form. *It is fair to give benefits to families of low-paid workers to help them out of poverty. However when these are withdrawn as income rises there is no incentive to work harder and earn more, so it is inefficient.*

There are no easy answers to the poverty trap.

The future of the welfare state
Throughout the 1950s and 60s there was cross-party consensus on the welfare state. In the 1970s the consensus was challenged from the Right by neo-liberals who wanted to 'roll back the state'. Their

arguments, together with rising unemployment, reawakened concern over costs and a 'dependency culture'.

The election of a Conservative government under Margaret Thatcher in 1979 led to debate on the future of the welfare state, but few measures to reduce its scope were taken until after the third Conservative election victory in 1988.

The debate continues (see the boxed item). Broadly there are two interrelated issues:

- the universalist 'one-nation' approach versus a means-tested 'safety net' system;
- the sustainability of the costs of provision.

Which position a voter or a politician takes depends more on their personal social philosophy than on the economics, statistics and

---

THE DEBATE ON THE FUTURE OF SOCIAL SECURITY

The principal arguments in favour of a reduced role for the state are:

- The government should confine itself to helping only those in need. Those who are able to look after themselves should do so by insuring themselves through the market to provide pensions for when they are old, and perhaps for when they are ill or unemployed.
- We can't afford it. People are not willing to pay the level of taxes and contributions necessary to keep the universal system going.

The main arguments for continuing at least a basic universal system, to which everyone contributes and receives benefits, are:

- Social solidarity. Those who support universalism argue in favour of a cooperative, as opposed to an individualist, approach to the provision of social welfare. They argue that if all members of society have a stake in the system they will wish to support it. If state benefits are reduced for the comfortable majority and are relied on mainly by the poor they will become stigmatized. People might become less willing to pay taxes and contributions to support benefits which do not apply to everyone.
- We can afford it. Projections ahead into the future, showing the proportion of GDP which would be taken by a universal benefits system show that it is sustainable and affordable.

projections that support their case. 'Fair play with the cake' is the basis of political differences between the parties and has to be addressed by voters each time there is a general election.

KEY WORDS

Social security	Income support
Education	Unemployment trap
Health care	Replacement rate
Public sector housing	Family credit
Cash transfers	Poverty trap
Merit goods	

Reading list
Hurl, B., Chapters 2 and 3 in *Privatization and the Public Sector*, 3rd edn, Heinemann Educational, 1995.
Smith, D., Chapter 3 in *UK Current Economic Policy*, Heinemann Educational, 1994.

Essay topics
1. 'The UK's taxation and welfare benefits systems have trapped the low-waged in relative poverty and the unwaged in unemployment.' Explain the causes of this situation. Explain how problems created by this situation might be reduced.
   [Associated Examining Board 1991]
2. A report published by the Rowntree Trust in 1995 concluded that the gap between the rich and the poor in the UK had increased since 1979.
   (a) How might the government use fiscal policy to reduce inequalities in income and wealth? [12 marks]
   (b) Discuss the impact of such policies upon both the pattern and the level of economic activity. [13 marks]
   [Associated Examining Board 1996]

Data Response Question
This task is based on a question set by the Associated Examining Board in 1996. Read the article, which is adapted from pieces in *The Economist* of 16 April and 3 September 1994, together with the figure which is adapted from *Fiscal Studies* in August 1991. Then answer the questions.

Minimum wages

Britain differs from most European Union countries and from America in having no statutory minimum wage.

Supporters of minimum wages say that they are needed to combat poverty among the low-paid. On the face of it, they would seem to help a significant number of workers. Around 5 per cent of full-time jobs pay less than £3.40 an hour before tax; more than 10 per cent of workers earn less than £4. Nearly 17 per cent of women get less than £4 an hour, compared with less than 8 per cent of men. One probably cleans your office. Another pulls your pint.

There is, though, an obvious objection to a minimum wage. It forces companies to pay more for their lowest-cost staff, which in theory should prompt them to shed jobs among the unskilled and the young. And some fear that minimum wages at the bottom then tempt higher-paid workers to push for higher pay for themselves, to restore wage differentials; that costs jobs further up the pay scales and may cause inflation.

The theory is probably right. By and large, empirical studies of the effects of minimum wages – most of which are based on American evidence – suggest that they do increase unemployment, especially among young people. But they do so at most only modestly; and the evidence is far from overwhelming.

Recent research suggests that, in certain circumstances, labour-market rigidities may prevent minimum wages from harming employment. David Card and Paul Krueger, two Princeton economists, looked at the effect, in 1992, of New Jersey raising its minimum wage from $4.25 to $5.05 an hour, while neighbouring Pennsylvania stuck to $4.25. They found that employment in the fast-food industry grew by 13 per cent more in New Jersey than it did in Pennsylvania.

This body of research shows that, in particular industries at particular times, a minimum wage might not destroy jobs. It could entice someone who lived on welfare to take a job. Better-paid employees might work harder and change jobs less frequently, while employers might invest more in their training.

This latest research does not convince everyone. Molly Meacher, a British economist, claimed that a national minimum wage would either have to be set at such a low level that it would be a mere token, or at a high enough level so that – as in France and Spain – it harmed employment. Among French workers aged under 26, one in four is out of a job. Economic growth in both France and Spain was under half that of Britain in 1993–94.

A minimum wage might also overcome the problem of the

'poverty trap' which discourages some of the unemployed from taking jobs, but job losses would limit the impact of minimum wages on poverty. Increased wages for some would come at the cost of joblessness for others. And, that aside, there is another good reason for not wanting a minimum wage. Often, the low-paid are not poor: according to the Institute for Fiscal Studies, a think-tank, a minimum wage would benefit mainly the wives of working husbands and young people living at home. The poor, more likely, are those who are not working at all. In families with dependent children where the husband is out of a job, only 1 per cent of wives work. Fewer than half of all lone mothers are employed.

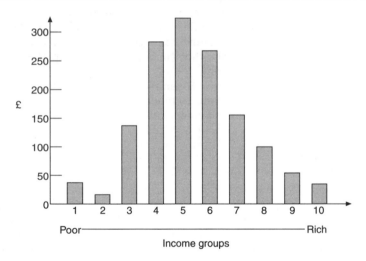

In the figure above, income group 1 represents the poorest 10 per cent of households in the UK, and so on.

1. Explain what is meant by a 'statutory minimum wage'. [2 marks]
2. Using economic analysis, explain why 'more than 10 per cent of (full-time) workers earn less than £4 (an hour)'. [4 marks]
3. Using a diagram, explain how the introduction of a minimum wage could raise the wages of low-paid workers. [4 marks]
4. Discuss the effects that the introduction of a minimum wage might have on poverty in the UK. [6 marks]
5. The information provided shows that the outcome of the introduction of a minimum wage is disputed. Discuss the effects such an introduction might have on employment and inflation in the UK economy. [9 marks]

Conclusion

'The market can be a good servant, but is often a bad master.'
John Eatwell

An economic system produces goods and services to satisfy human wants. The market does this and, though imperfect, it is the best system yet to emerge to answer the basic *what?*, *how?* and *for whom?* questions.

Markets determine prices. Prices direct production, telling producers which goods are in demand and where demands are changing. Markets also determine the prices of resources – labour, capital etc. – and profit-seeking producers are guided to minimize production costs. Incomes earned in resource (factor) markets give people the power to buy the economy's output.

We need some criteria to determine whether markets are working or failing. These criteria are that the outcomes of the system should be both *efficient* and *equitable*.

The outcome is efficient if welfare is maximized. The output from given inputs must be at a maximum – productive efficiency – and that output must be in line with what people want. This is *allocative or Pareto efficiency*, and the conditions that achieve it were set out in Chapter 1: for any good, marginal social cost must equal marginal social benefit. A variety of circumstances, from monopoly to external effects, may prevent this. When Pareto efficiency is achieved it is not possible to make one consumer better off without worsening the position of another.

Efficiency takes no account of the distribution of income. If society consisted of rich Arthur and poor Ben, and if it were not possible to make poor Ben better off without worsening rich Arthur's position, then the situation would be Pareto-efficient.

We therefore need another criterion for judging economic outcomes,

'You may want shoes but I need a tax cut'

and that criterion is equity. Equity is about the distribution of the economy's output, about social justice. It is more difficult to define because there is no objective measure.

When policy is assessed or when policy changes are proposed they are judged in terms of whether they are efficient and fair, or in terms of a trade-off between the two objectives. This book has attempted to do this for several important issues – monopoly and competition; external costs; external benefits, including public goods; supply side economics; the welfare state.

Sometimes there is conflict between efficiency and equity. For example, reducing income tax and increasing VAT may make for more work effort and higher output, which is efficient. But it also makes tax more regressive, weighing more heavily on poorer people, which can be considered inequitable. Unemployment benefit provides incomes, which is fair, but may also reduce incentives to work, which is inefficient.

Some policy changes, however, increase both equity and efficiency. For example, reducing monopoly power raises output towards the competitive level, which is efficient, and reduces consumer exploitation, which is fair. Subsidizing bus fares would increase the use of public transport and reduce pollution and congestion, and increase the real incomes of the relatively poor who are the heaviest users of public transport.

It is possible to assess any change in economic policy according to its efficiency and equity effects. The aim of this book has been to show how to do it. It has demonstrated that welfare economics – assessing market failure and policies to remedy it – is simply *applied microeconomics*. It has tried to demonstrate, too, that microeconomics is not merely an interesting intellectual exercise (or not, according to your taste), but can be applied to the real world and its problems. It can help us to think more clearly about the market system, its successes and its failures. Its techniques can be used to judge measures that governments take to try to improve things – those measures which try to turn the market into 'a good servant'.

Index